The Proof is in the Poodle

The Proof is in the Poodle

One Veterinarian's Exploration into Healing

Donna Kelleher, DVM

Two Harbors Press

Two Harbors Press
212 3ʳᵈ Avenue North, Suite 290
Minneapolis, MN 55401
612.455.2293
www.TwoHarborsPress.com

ISBN-13: 978-1-937928-06-3
LCCN: 2011943984

Distributed by Itasca Books

Printed on 100% post-consumer recycled paper. Some proceeds from this
book sales will go to United Plant Savers (www.unitedplantsavers.org) and
WeSNip (www.wesnip.org). See the website www.proofisinthepoodle.com
for more information.

Printed in the United States of America

"Out beyond ideas of wrong-doing and right-doing, there is a field. I'll meet you there."

—Rumi

This book is dedicated to the memory of veterinarian, herbalist and author Juliette de Baïracli Levy, whose spirit still wanders the colorful gardens of herbalists everywhere in search of the perfect medicine.

Author's Note:

As the subtitle of this book suggests, the following pages represent an exploration into the idea of physical, emotional and spiritual healing for both our animals and ourselves. Although some of the names have been changed and a few of the humans are composite characters, the stories are essentially true. May they touch your heart as they still touch mine.

Contents

Prelude

IN MY OFFICE, an aging golden retriever named Jasper sits by my fax machine and waits for his latest ultrasound report. But I already know the results from a gentle wag of his tail and his rejuvenated appetite: the cancer is in remission. Unlike an oncologist, I don't *treat* cancer. I focus instead on healing the patient's failing immune system; Jasper's gave rise to two large liver tumors. I worried that Jasper would succumb to one of his bleed-outs, or pass away after his severe reaction to a pain patch. But in each instance, a force rallied inside him, a spirit that science cannot yet quantify, and he beat the odds.

For eighteen years, I've been using safe, effective therapies to treat animals like Jasper. Even while attending veterinary school, I looked beyond our clinical training to a world of healing that was older than my young imagination could carry me, to the world of acupuncture and Chinese medicine. Here, I found my calling and kinship among fellow healers, veterinarians who thought like I did, who believed the body possessed the inner vitality and physiologic mechanisms to heal itself. Now I could heal animals suffering from chronic pain with just a few acupuncture treatments.

But there were always those challenging cases for which I needed to learn a new modality, leading me to seek out ongoing training in gentle chiropractic techniques and soft-tissue manipulation. My goal was always the same: no matter how many years of chronic disease accumulated in my patient, I strived to alleviate it without pharmaceutical intervention.

All along the way, my patients' humans were a key part of this process. The road to recovery wasn't as simple as administering a pill twice a day. Most of the time, clients had extensive homework and without their willingness to take on an integral role in their pets' therapy, success might not have been possible. When I encouraged clients to understand each step of the healing process, to make specific, homemade and balanced diets, to perform daily massage and physical therapy techniques and employ precise exercise regimes, their old dogs recuperated and bounded around like puppies again.

Over the years, my practice expanded to include severe autoimmune disease, digestive distress and organ failure. In the treatment of these more difficult diseases, I frequently found botanical herbal cures to be at the center of my therapy. The vital enzymes in plants triggered my patients' mammalian genes in a highly-evolved and unique way. I began to realize that by prescribing botanical remedies and stimulating these complex genetic relationships, a deep reservoir of vibrant health could be tapped.

Treating patients with herbal medications is a skill I learned, not in veterinary school, but in the mountains and open fields, digging roots, picking flowers and preparing medicines by the light of the sun and moon. Early on, my herbal teachers were patient when I clung to my dogmatic Western training. I eventually learned to take in their lessons of plant spirit healing while still valuing and continuing my conventional medical education as well, for every truth is only a half-truth and every reality is tiered, multi-faceted and always changing. Animals already know this and embrace it.

Although I have learned from some wonderful and famous herbalists, many of my most important teachers have been the animals, both the ones that I work with in my practice as well as my own dogs and horses. In the following pages, I'll introduce you to these animals, my real teachers, and also to the hidden truths that they have helped me to see.

My path began long before I met a little horse named Tino, or a small black terrier named Smudge, or Sampson, a scruffy poodle mutt who followed me home after school one day.

Many years ago, it all started as an obsession with anything that had fur.

Growing Up with Fur

"So, this surprise . . ." My mother paused, as if she could put her job as college professor on hold. "Does it have hair?"

I often timed my attempts to slide in another stray animal right before final exams, just when my mom's defenses were weakest as hundreds of stressed-out political science students clanged at her office door. It was cheating. But I didn't feel guilty.

I looked down, evaluating the stray who had followed me home from school. Peering up at me were two soft brown eyes, an elongated muzzle, four paws and an occasional twitch of a scruffy tail. But rather than a beautiful plush coat, scraps of white tufts sprouted from the dog's blotchy skin like patches in an old tattered quilt. I answered, "Well, not really."

I heard only silence as she contemplated the possibilities—an amphibian, a snake, or even worse, a water turtle with a tank the size of a swimming pool needing tri-weekly cleanings. But even now, with her mind on the world's fragile political conflicts, she called my bluff. "Donna, I already told you. No more animals."

"I swear, this time it's not my fault. He followed me home. I tried to ignore him." At the end of 1980, six months after Mount St. Helens erupted, we moved to Washington State. My mom, brother, our basset mix named Julietta, and I left my father and Boston's flat landscape and drove a rickety moving truck across the country towards our new home just south of Seattle. As we crossed the Cascades, I felt as if I had entered another world. Julietta and I gazed up in wonder at the mysterious mountains all around us. With their peaks seemingly in the heavens, I couldn't tell where mountain ended and cloud began. After many hours of consideration, I decided that the snow-capped vestige of Mount St. Helens looked like Julietta's lower molar.

Our new home was tucked away in a cul-de-sac, flanked by a forested greenbelt, and it soon became a rest stop for gnarly runts and cockeyed tomcats looking for a safe place to hunker down at night. Taking them to the Humane Society may have seemed the reasonable thing to do, but we were Kellehers, a stubborn Irish bunch with a survivalist attitude of do-it-yourself even if it killed you. This applied to everything from moving furniture to rewiring your house to rescuing animals.

The bedraggled little poodle sat squarely at my feet, awaiting his fate and panting nervously when our bossy tabby, Tigger, strutted towards him sideways, hair follicles plugged up in attack mode. The hairless, scruffy dog who I later named Sampson when no one responded to our *Found—Bald Dog* signs, was fifteen pounds tops, fragile and mild-mannered. He wasn't the first dog I'd brought home, not even the first bald one, and yet there was something special about him and his soft spirit. He belonged with us. And that was that. A resigned hush was my mom's final response, so I knew I could keep him. Cat or dog, rat or hamster, it didn't matter. Each hard-won victory ended up in the bathtub, my way of celebrating.

I hoisted Sampson into the warm water, streams running between his ribs, sheets of soothing soap frothing down his legs and gathering at his feet. He blinked two or three times as I knelt beside him. Looking back, I probably appeared equally pitiful: a scrawny girl who barely dragged a brush through her long, thick hair. But I groomed the animals as though they were royalty. I wore an old dungaree apron and filled the pockets with the essentials: a pair of nail trimmers, a rusty flea comb and a few elongated cotton-tipped ear swabs. By the end of the bath, I was as wet as my patient.

Sampson looked up at me, curious about all the attention. I plucked smatterings of black discharge from the corners of his eyes, checked his ears for mites and combed over his rump, looking for signs of fleas. I investigated every nook and cranny, leaning over my subject until my back ached. I didn't want even one parasite to escape, lest my mother put the kibosh on my new dog.

This ritual with my newfound strays commonly resulted in bruises on my knees, scratches on my arms and water running down my apron and splattering in my face. After grooming, I'd admire the combed-out new addition to our household as you would a flower garden after a day of weeding. But this particular poodle's bath only served to uncover additional red blotches, making my new dog appear even more tattered, with no remaining dirt to hide the evidence.

As I toweled him off, I looked past his pustules to the possible champion that might emerge from this unwanted pooch. He might become a prized cancer-sniffer and save hundreds of people. We'd convince Westminster to start a mutt class. Then, we'd win every show. Despite the scattered, patchy tufts of fur, I imagined a valuable variety of poodle, the type a rich lady might tuck under her arm on the way to the hairdresser.

Other thirteen-year-old girls didn't understand. While it seemed perfectly normal for me to spend a lunch hour reaching into a dumpster to pluck out a feral kitten that would show its appreciation by scratching my arm and expressing its anal glands onto my shirt, girls at school were more apt to primp their hair in front of the mirror. While they spent the weekend trolling the mall for boys, I worked at a local stable in exchange for riding lessons. I cleaned stalls, swept aisles and scrubbed buckets, happily picking stones from hooves, probing for signs of thrush and cultivating a lifelong addiction to the smell of horses.

As long as they came from an animal and not a person, bodily excretions from any orifice were handled like a cluster of crumbs from a morning muffin. Yes, you needed to wipe them off, but there was no hurry. A smear of blood on my shirt from my cat's infected tooth was a badge of honor, as was the small patch of diarrhea on my pant leg from a nervous rat. It was nothing to get worked up over.

Fighting my animal-rescuing tendencies was a losing battle and my mom knew it. I was already on my life's path—first as a horse trainer and then, later, as a holistic veterinarian. My family might have preferred that I end up like my brother, Neil, who would become fluent in German prior to working on the Human Proteome Project. But instead, I fought for my rescued band of misfits: Tigger, our brown tabby; Cirrus, a long-haired white cat; Dolly Madison, an elegant black cat; Shadow, a Siamese the neighbors could hear howl at feeding time; Julietta, a basset mix who would follow me up ladders and down slides; and Rufus

Aspirilla, a suicidal but ironically long-lived teddy bear hamster. It was here that most people became bored with my list of animals, so I usually stopped before I got to the goldfish: Loretta, Dimples and Jill.

I found most of my dogs and cats under a random hedge or through a neighbor, but I collected my rodents at an unlikely hubbub of animal adoption—the dentist's office—sometime before the numb lower lip and the nifty new toothbrush. Once, another kid's mom threatened to return her two small rats to the pet store. "I told you we have too many animals," she complained in the waiting room. Immediately, I felt a kinship with the girl. We were victims of a great adult conspiracy. The girl hid her face in her hands the way I did when the world seemed violent and unfair. That's when I piped up.

"Hey, do your rats need a home?" I asked. My mother looked up from *The Economist* and lightly knocked me on the arm with the rolled-up magazine, the way we reprimanded a puppy for peeing in the house before clickers and high-pitched baby talk became the norm. I whispered back, "Come on, Mom, you can't let some boa constrictor get those rats."

"When you leave home someday, guess who gets stuck with all these critters?" Mom said. For as long as we could remember, Neil and I knew that, at age eighteen, she'd kick us out of the house and out of the country. She frequently lectured us about the merits of

6

living and working abroad. Africa. The Middle East. Europe. South America. It didn't matter if there were dangers in the world, my mother ignored them all, traipsing off to Macedonia or Southeast Asia. A traveling chameleon, she happily blended into any culture. Years later, I'd choose to do social work in England, and my brother would study chemistry in Germany on a Fulbright scholarship.

"I'll find a home for everyone. Even the goldfish," I promised.

The next day a pale girl came to the front door delivering my new rats, Safire and Aphrodite. Safire ran circles around my bed as though it were an Olympic track and she, the star athlete, while Aphrodite sat on my lap tucking her nose under my elbow, allowing me to scratch the top of her head. I inspected her small toes. They were as thin as toothpicks, but incredibly adept at numerous activities including holding my finger in a rat handshake.

"How about those piano lessons?" Mom asked, hoping to phase out the animals in favor of a hobby that did not wag, chortle, whine or get into expensive mischief. But I just scowled at the array of inanimate musical instruments as they sat there, lifeless, propped up on walls or smack-dab in the middle of the living room. Piano. Recorder. Flute. I tried them one by one. I disregarded the violin too, opting instead to read my music teacher's encyclopedia of dog breeds during those times when she was preoccupied with a phone call. I downright objected to gymnastics, a sport designed to waste my time while, back at home, my hairy band of rescues hungrily awaited their dinner.

My mother had to live with my obsession and the inevitable repercussions: listening to a new poodle's loud snoring at the bottom of her bed, rescuing the occasional renegade goldfish flopping around on the floor, missing important business calls thanks to the three cats curled up on her lap. But the most unnerving episodes happened when Rufus would escape from his cage and scamper across the kitchen floor heading for the safety of the refrigerator. In a sleepless attempt to safeguard him from the prowling cats, we'd take turns camping out next to the stove. Eventually, Rufus would hobble over, all covered with a dusty filth, and peer up at us with beady, dehydrated eyes.

Mom tried to hide her love for animals, but she owed her life to a pair of brown draft horses, Tom and Jerry. Bleary-eyed after drinking too much dandelion wine the previous night, Uncle Everett snapped his whip at the two horses early one summer morning, trying to get them to move the manure spreader forward. But on this particular morning, the horses stood motionless, refusing to move. Another crack of the whip. Again, no response. As Jerry turned his head to look back, Everett noticed a flash of pink between the horse's giant hooves. Suddenly, he realized that my two-year-old mother had been playing under the horses' legs. My grandmother found young Mom covered with hay and barn soot as she reached up on tiptoes to touch the horses' soft noses. Tom and Jerry became instant family heroes for standing their ground.

Perhaps my mom feared most that, if my hobby went unbridled, the number of beasts might escalate in size and number. And to a certain extent, her fears were realized. Each cat or dog made way for another with a tacit understanding that there was always room for one more. Most of the drama around my menagerie came in the form of what they left behind: urine out of the box, fecal balls found in the back of a coat closet, or worse, in a shoe. Worst of all, there was fur. Tail hair, pin hair, soft and coarse varieties. All discovered in unlikely spots and subject to our scrutiny.

"Whose is this?" Neil asked, plucking a hair from his shirt.

"I don't know. Dolly's?" I guessed as I fought with the vacuum cleaner. Shedding season sent the machine into a sputter of uselessness, so I stretched my index finger deep inside the thing, as far as I could reach, to clean out the wads of hair. When a flashlight revealed even more clumps, I used my mom's favorite pen to scoop out its inner chambers. I thought I could hear the vacuum gasp from the closet whenever a new animal came home, doubtful that I, and I alone, could keep up with the brushing.

Animal hair clung to our clothes, got in our eyes and noses, dangled from lamps, clumped together and rolled around in the corners. Stray hair got into our food sometimes, but my brother and I paid no attention to it. On meatloaf nights, bits of white, soft undercoat floated into dinner like an airborne condiment, a bland straw-like version of saffron. My brother and I looked at one another and he nonchalantly mouthed, "Cirrus," shrugging off our fluffy white cat's generous donation to dinner.

Sometimes my obsession with four-leggeds backfired on me. On Christmas Day, 1981, the first and last time our British aunt visited us from New York, a three-inch whisker lurking between her gravy and mashed potatoes nearly shut down the holiday.

Aunt Myrtle had short crimped hair, a pointy nose and an upper lip that protruded like a parrot's beak, especially when she grew disgruntled. To us, she resembled an ornery green-winged Macaw. She traveled with her own cup, saucer and special tea, no doubt clinging to it for sanity. The tea was the loose leaf variety, sold only in England and strong as battery acid. I marveled at the way she delicately tucked her bony forefinger along the cup's handle, never actually holding the thing. Somehow, it stayed with her, through magnetism, I thought. She clutched her saucer as though it were the Old World, some distant place full of green hills dotted with wooly white sheep and thatched roofs. Aunt Myrtle regarded paper products with disdain, instead using a folded set of hand-tatted colorful handkerchiefs. Since her arrival to our home, she occupied herself with solitaire, shuffling her favorite deck of cards.

I amused myself with her resemblance to the Queen. She also kept busy by plucking cat hairs from her tweed coat, eventually deciding that standing was easier than dealing with the disarray that was our couch—a piece of furniture with at least one full undercoat.

Aunt Myrtle snubbed all the animals except Sampson. Mom thought it was his lack of hair that attracted her. I watched carefully as he persistently broke down her defenses, getting under her skin and working his way into her cold heart. Silence and a gentle glare were Sampson's ammunition and he cast both her way. I don't know why he tried so hard with Aunt Myrtle when the rest of us just wanted to ignore her. Perhaps it was his way of licking her wounds, traumas incurred by a life of hard knocks. Finally, at the end of the afternoon, when she thought no one was looking, Aunt Myrtle slowly bent over to pet him, her frail fingers softly gliding over his head.

My mother decorated the dining table with green holly and beautiful red flowers even though it was just a picnic table and we were sitting on benches. Throughout the day, Mom peeled potatoes, mashed yams and rolled out all the piecrusts. When it was ready, she placed all the food on the table and exhaled, relieved to have finished grading papers and cooking dinner all in one day.

It was at that moment, with everyone quietly chewing their food and my aunt chattering on about bombs in London, that the whisker caught her in mid-sentence. She gagged and choked and coughed as if a lump of turkey or a clump of bread had been the perpetrator. I wondered how she'd ever breathe again. But then, as she gasped and grew gruesomely rigid, the dreaded culprit slowly emerged from between her front teeth. She pinched the whisker between thumb and forefinger and held it to the light.

My brother looked at me knowing I was in deep trouble. As if Tigger had brought a mouse head in the house, my mom turned as red and coarse as a cat's tongue and shot me a look that said, "If any of these animals so much as pass gas, you're going to your room until February."

If the whisker had landed on my brother's plate or my own, we would have simply wiped it to the side. But Aunt Myrtle raised a hand to her forehead, threatened to pass out, and made me sit beside her on the couch, dabbing her neat handkerchief into cool water and then onto her forehead. It was like purgatory, this gentle dabbing; I'd much rather have clipped a lion's nails or cleaned a shark tank or even expressed a wolf's anal glands.

I would have been happy to toss the whisker away, to conceal the evidence, but Neil had other ideas. After what seemed like lifetimes of scientific investigation, he deduced that the whisker, which was three inches long, sharp and black, must have come from Julietta's muzzle. From under the picnic table, she lifted her head innocently at the mention of her name.

Where school was concerned, even with a crippling case of the flu and no sleep, Neil would still ace any exam, an absent-minded chemistry professor in the making. But in regard to the animals, even Neil deferred to my opinion, particularly because he held a bad track record with anything that had fur.

It was Neil who would lose Sampson in a snowstorm, a dog normally glued to our heels. "How can you lose a dog?" I asked, muttering a reminder about the invention of the leash. I finally found Sampson several blocks away in a garage, evidently held for safekeeping.

My brother was no stranger to equine accidents, either. One day, Flicka bucked him off into a beehive, his torso covered with painful stings. He recovered just long enough to have even more bad fortune. Flicka decided to launch into a full gallop, with Neil screaming and clutching to her mane. In a show of great pony fortitude, she suddenly halted at a pond, causing Neil to somersault over the top of her head. He landed in a patch of soggy scum that any self-respecting frog would reject. When he finally returned to the house, his face was still covered with a green sticky slime, the only thing that held his broken eyeglasses to his forehead.

Life herded Neil inside, first to shower off strings of green algae, and later, into a windowless laboratory where his own discoveries were to be made. But it herded me outside to retrieve Neil's loose

13

pony by an algae-ridden pond, and then, years later, to search out and study medicinal herbs in the moss-covered rainforests of the Pacific Northwest.

A New Mentor

THE OLD LADY from down the street was a crazy coot. At least, that's what the neighbors thought of her. She lived at the end of a long driveway, her faded peach house shrouded by conifers, each one surrounded with a circle of native plants. People did not care that she knew about plants. They only noticed that her grey hair straggled about, as though it had not been combed in weeks, and that her colorful fashion choices provided an unwelcome glow to our bland suburban neighborhood. Rather than politely playing a nice game of bridge and quietly taking her medications, she spoke up at board meetings and protested against any proposed developments that might harm the local environment.

The neighbors investigated her comings and goings,

suspiciously eyeing her between the broad wood slats of her fence. I saw the postman stop in his tracks when she cavorted in her fuchsia corduroys and gold blouse. Although he was normally a quiet sort of fellow, when pressed by Mrs. Barney across the street, he'd release just enough tidbits to keep the gossip going. To the old lady, clothes were just another way people could judge her, so there were times she'd try going without them. When the neighbors complained, and they usually did, she'd half-heartedly comply, rebelling with loud colors, her blouse unbuttoned lower than deemed appropriate for her age. It's not as if she had any special physical attributes. She was just born into the wrong culture at the wrong time.

Back then, the old woman provided me with job security, as she was one of the few paying clients to answer my newspaper ad. That first morning, I walked up her garden path and saw her frantically digging up weeds to clear out a patch of irises, dirt flying in every direction. Her silver blouse sparkled in the midday sun. Interrupting her, I said, "Hi. I'm Donna Kelleher. You answered my ad in the paper."

"Oh, yes," she replied, rubbing her palms on her apron. "I need someone to help me with the weeding." We talked about how much she would pay me and when I would start. As I turned to leave, I asked her, "By the way, what's your name?"

"I've been called many things over the years," she said, chuckling as she closely examined an earthworm before nestling it back into the soil.

I looked at the beautiful flowers at her feet, their blue reflective of a sobering beauty in the old woman's eyes. "I think I'd like to call you Iris." The name must have stuck because she never asked me to call her anything else.

In the fall I raked leaves and needles, and in the spring I planted seeds and fresh new starts. As the summer progressed, she taught me how to recognize common weeds: a buttercup in its early stages or couch grass when it still resembled a dead white root. "Well, aren't you a crawdaddy out of water?" she'd say to the moisture-born horsetail as it attempted to root into a dry mound of soil. Then she'd hurl it into her silver bucket. We would crimp back the columbine to encourage the growth of new flowers. Teetering atop ladders, we pruned her unruly rhododendrons to a manageable height of ten feet, filling a whole row of composting bags. The idea that she'd ever trust me to do these things by myself seemed farfetched. But within two seasons, that's just what happened.

My mother reported that, back in the seventeenth century, Iris might have been burned at the stake, if not for her defiant lack of fashion, then for her unusual relationship to plants. But since the old lady only had a couple of spayed cats, my mom appreciated that she would at least not be a source of more animals. My only complaint was the lady's request that I start at seven on Saturday mornings. Although I could pedal to her house in less than five minutes, I still needed Tigger's wake-up paw to get me there on time, which seemed to somehow match Iris's internal clock, as though both were magically synchronized.

6:00 a.m. I feel a cat's paw, half-dollar-sized, soft as a pussy willow, gently tap my face. 6:03 a.m. Tigger's paw presses into my cheekbone or below my eye, the pressure applied consistently for the next several minutes. 6:06 a.m. My eyes pop open to sharp claws expanding into my cheek, emitting a gentle warning: *you will now get up and feed me.* 6:10 a.m. I open my eyes, only to see two big, satisfied green cat eyes with long, languid, slit-like pupils staring at me. *Breakfast at long last!*

One such Saturday, I walked to Iris's house with my new bald poodle mutt, Sampson, his weeping skin sores still oozing along his backbone. At night he'd lick them open. Then the coughing started. Two trips to the vet and a course of antibiotics did little to relieve his symptoms. When his nightly hacking grew worse, I would lurch out of bed, holding him close under the covers so no one else would wake up. I kept an eye on him with a flashlight under the sheets; in its glare, he resembled a gangly, disproportionate bear. As Sampson and I walked up Iris's long driveway, new smells filled his nostrils. His nose was one with the earth. Her two cats greeted us with their feline display of defensiveness, backbones arched, hair on end and eyes blazing. But Sampson didn't seem to notice. All his attention went into sniffing the purple and gold pansies, curled up in the morning chill.

"What do we have here? Another runaway?" My hobby was no secret to the neighborhood, nor to Iris. "He looks as sad as a wet hen." Her glasses slid down the bridge of her nose as she considered the poodle, grey waves of hair falling about her shoulders. A single wart peeked out from a crease along her mouth, a blemish that had gradually been replaced, to my eye, with her more endearing qualities. I looked down and saw her tabby cats cavorting about the garden. The darker of the two had black stripes stretching lengthwise to her tail. Iris called her Tinkerbelle, owing to her unique desire to explore bell-shaped flowers. When the cat wasn't nuzzling her nose and whiskers into a blue comfrey flower, she'd lie across the garden eyeing it, her tail thumping the ground.

Iris examined Sampson, gently pinching and stretching his skin as though she were milking pollen from one of her magnificent honeysuckles. She spent a long time looking closely at his moist red skin sores. I could tell by the determined look on her face that she could help him. We began gathering specific herbs from her garden, differentiating their leaves and flowers and rubbing our fingers along their roots, searching for qualities I considered mysterious. *What was she looking for?* I thought, following her like a hungry kitten, watching closely as she'd reject one flower in favor of another, both seemingly equal in color, size and texture.

We picked orange and yellow flowers, snipped golden rhizomes and pinched off the thick watery base of a plant with small bristles that left me with itchy red bumps. Weeks earlier, while sweeping her patio, I watched through Iris's kitchen window as she administered a straw-yellow tea into Tinkerbelle's mouth. The cat had suffered from the high fever of a severe infection and Iris's tea gradually transformed the weak, lethargic kitty into a picture of health: Tinkerbelle was back to rolling in the catnip within one week.

That day, as Iris mumbled something about Sampson's dry cough, she introduced me to mullein, a plant as tall as a scarecrow. I was hard-pressed to forget it, with its large leaf stalks resembling the arms of a saguaro cactus. Numerous yellow flowers covered the end of each thick stem. We clipped its leaves, which were smooth as felt, and used them to prepare an infusion to soothe Sampson's irritated lungs. Once we soaked the leaves in hot water, they released a cascade of slimy demulcent chemicals that would moisten Sampson's dry lung tissue. The idea that a tea taken internally could affect all the mucous membranes of the body was completely foreign to me. But Iris was convinced that Sampson's dry cough would improve by adding the tea to his food, as it strengthened his body's own natural mucosal immunity. I shrugged. If the old woman had given me muddy puddle water, I would have tried that too.

Iris boiled well water in an old, curved-spout kettle while she put me to work pulling dandelions. Instead of tossing the yellow-flowered weeds, she carefully rinsed and baked them. "Roasted dandelion root is the best medicine," she'd often say, drinking dandelion tea instead of coffee, but I wondered about her sanity when I saw the rest of the neighborhood declaring war on the beautiful plants, spraying them with gallons of chemicals. Even my mom dug them up half-heartedly on semester breaks. If they were so healthy, why didn't everybody else see it?

At night when I worried about Sampson's symptoms and was unable to sleep, I thought of Iris, harvesting nettles with her bare hands and somehow not getting stung. Her knowledge of plant medicine extended far beyond what was contained in any textbook. As I watched Iris confidently navigate her herbal garden, there was something oddly familiar about her. I felt very comfortable in a forest with her, searching for Indian plum buds to unfurl, the first sign of spring. She also had a way with animals, whose opinions I respected far more than those of the neighbors. So despite her unorthodox behaviors, I trusted her.

The very neighbors who gossiped about Iris occasionally came to seek her help when no one else was looking. One day, as I pretended to trim the bleeding hearts, Mrs. Barney's cousin wandered up the driveway with a large bandage over his right hand. The man was a carpenter by trade but had no medical insurance.

He explained that he had accidentally cut into the tip of his finger a week earlier. Although he had kept the cut clean and wrapped, the pain increased as infection set in.

He unwrapped his hand, revealing a purple and swollen index finger, but Iris seemed most concerned about the chalky black appearance of its tip. As the man sat in a folding metal lawn chair holding his ailing hand, Iris and I began working on a cure. We collected her prized white yarrow, carefully cutting two sprigs of its green lacy leaves with each flowering umbel. Using her wide marble mortar and pestle, I crushed the flowers and leaves, pushing my weight into the medicine.

We created a potent, darkly colored tea, the likes of which watered the eyes, forcing all the cats to sit up and take notice. She handed a bowl of it to the man, instructing him to soak his finger six times a day, carefully drying it between treatments. She also made him promise to eat a healthy diet, including fresh citrus fruit, raw vegetables and Brazil nuts, "for vitamin C, selenium and protein," she whispered. I studied the way she chose her treatments, one hand grasping for tried and true garden remedies and the other reaching towards an ethereal healing place, as though directed by someone or something intangible even to her. She seemed to look beyond her garden to visualize the cure. Over the next two weeks, the flesh color slowly returned to the man's finger, eventually healing with only a scar to tell the tale. "If you can't see the cure, if you can't even imagine it, then it can't happen," she later told me.

But when crotchety Mr. Barney, an old drunk with an intolerance to pain medications, wandered into Iris's garden looking for a cure for his hangover, she flatly refused to help him. I remember Mr. Barney slumped under a Sitka willow, his feet planted in the meadowsweet, the powerful salicylate-containing plant that gave rise to aspirin. He couldn't have been closer to the herbs he was looking for if they jumped up and bit him in the behind. "Leave the bottle alone," Iris said, ignoring the will of the willow and the meadowsweet. "That'll cure you." She was tough and I admired her for that. She'd help almost anyone for free. But if a person's symptoms were a product of their own self-abuse, or part of the normal healing process, she would stubbornly refuse care. "Sometimes the best way to help is not to help at all," she said.

We made Sampson's wound-healing tea from what I'd later know to be Oregon grape, calendula, comfrey and plantain. It smelled no better or worse than any of Iris's other teas, and yet my poodle mutt did not resist his treatments. He stood quietly each misty morning as I applied the tea to his skin; amazingly, he lapped up the mullein infusion with his food. One morning my mom asked, "So what did Iris do this time?" I thought of the way the old lady knelt on the earth, how the sun reflected on her silver sparkling skirt, and how she carefully selected each petal and leaf. I loved leaning over the steaming pot of melting sweet flowers, leaves and roots. Her cats lollygagged about, purring as the air filled with the scent of the steamy elixir, the end of their tails flicking with new energy. In my mind, Iris didn't soar on a broomstick but blasted in on gale-force winds, leaving a soft breeze of angelic healing in her wake.

"Oh, it was just another tea," I said, keeping Iris's secrets to myself.

Choices

IN MY EARLY TWENTIES, during my summer breaks from college on the East Coast, I returned home to Washington to visit my family. Occasional summer evenings I spent with my friends, trapping feral cats and transporting them to the Humane Society to be spayed or neutered. We would camp out by the railroad tracks, watch our traps, drink peppermint schnapps and listen to hushed Def Leppard from my car stereo. As we gazed into the night, we felt satisfied that we were doing our small part in decreasing the number of unwanted litters.

Ten years later, I came to realize that I didn't want a litter either. While most of my friends were attending birthing classes, only a few of us remained with our hissing wild cats, their green eyes glowing in the dark under the light of a full moon. When I was thirty-five years old, I decided to have a tubal ligation. My friends tried their best to change my mind. They would hold up tiny tie-dyed tee shirts, prematurely cooing to excite my interest in reproduction. I tried to want kids. I really did. But it just didn't feel like me.

"Come on, Donna, snap out of it," one of them said with the forceful nature of an intervention, shortly before I was to go in for the procedure. "This decision is permanent, you know. It's hard to reverse." We sat together at a loud, busy pub in downtown Seattle. Everywhere I looked, I saw no shortage of people. Although my friend had a rocky, unstable marriage, another kid was on his way. I quickly steered the conversation away from my oviducts, grateful that she did not call me selfish. Another friend had attempted that argument the week before.

"Who will take care of you when you're old?" my friend continued, and I thought of Wiltshire, England, where I had volunteered at various nursing homes when I was eighteen years old. Playing dominos, clipping toenails, and making lunch for the residents occupied my time. Rather than being sedated, open-mouthed and mindless in front of television screens, these nursing home residents were fully conscious of how infrequently their family members visited. On holidays, I'd see a half dozen of them, grey-haired and slumped in their wheelchairs, waiting by the window for hours, just in case a family member, *anyone's* son or daughter, stopped by.

I had always known that I didn't want children and that a life of animal care awaited me. As a young veterinarian, I had not changed my mind. It wasn't that I hated kids. I admired my niece's tiny hands and feet, all curled up as she slept. "Well," I admitted, "she does kind of resemble a baby yellow Lab." My family understood this as a compliment, although they also knew I preferred the puppy.

I found my laparoscopic surgeon by way of an Italian greyhound named Bella who had a stubborn autoimmune disease. Bella required regular acupuncture treatments at least twice a month to keep her symptoms under control, so her human and I had a lot of time to talk about our lives. That's when I learned that Bella's owner had fibroids the size of lemons, which had amazingly been removed through two small pinhole incisions on either side of her navel. She held Bella with one arm and lifted her shirt slightly to show off what we came to call her non-scar. I wanted that surgeon for my procedure too.

I arrived for my consultation appointment and immediately noticed the heavy stale odor of antiseptics. When I was young, my farming family described hospitals as "prep schools for the dyin'." They were the last place we saw my old aunts and uncles before they wound up in a casket. So over the last two weeks, I had settled all my affairs and had my will notarized. That day, I signed nine surgical forms, each one stating that I knew well ahead of time that a grueling and potentially painful death was a possible surgical outcome. But what the surgeon actually said to me was simpler, and less sinister: "I can remove virtually any organ in your body laproscopically." I thought about all the organs that I was still using.

"Oh, that's nice," I said. "But let's just stick to the ligation."

Then, more serious, the doctor folded his hands in his lap. "You *really* don't want kids? You're still pretty young, and a lot of docs just wouldn't do it."

"It would be hard to juggle parenthood, work and animals," I said, and thought of my friend Lisa, whose Labrador was relegated to the back yard after her son was born. Her horse now hung his head as he stared at a new swing set just outside his paddock.

Later that day, I spoke with a fellow veterinarian, Jeff Blake, and told him about my decision. Jeff had been a friend for years and had supported me through many difficult times. "I think that is great. As always, you believe in something and you're truly committed to it." I viewed Jeff as a kayaking or hiking partner but had long ago decided he was not boyfriend material. He was too nice for that. And he went to bed way too early.

Instead, I found boyfriends on the tango floor. I was attracted most of all to the dance itself. Unfortunately, the romantic nature of the music would often cast a spell over me, throwing off what little sense I had. I fell for Lorenzo's warm smile and dark features as we intertwined our legs at the knees, spinning into a *gancho*. His belief in monogamy was shaky and, over the months we spent together, he taught me the importance of integrity by showing me what life would be like without it. The only thing we really had in common, other than dancing, was our mutual unspoken need to change one another. While I wanted him to fall more in love with my dogs than with me, he hoped he could change my mind about not wanting children. I found him staring at passing strollers, even though I was perfectly happy to settle into a routine of morning dog walks, a half-dozen biodegradable bags adorning my belt. Before we amiably parted ways, a relief to both of us, he agreed to transport me to and from the hospital for my procedure.

"Now, don't forget, if I die, you know where my will is," I said, recounting my last-minute wishes.

"Don't be negative," he ordered.

"I'm not negative. I just want to be prepared," I answered in a calm voice, all the while feeling my stomach grip with worry. We drove across the West Seattle Bridge towards Pill Hill, an avenue where half a dozen medical institutions corrupted the skyline, panels of glass as tall as the eye could see.

I told the nurse who checked me in that this was my spay day. "After all the cats I've fixed, it's only fair," I smiled. But Lorenzo felt it was his place to clarify my intention: "Actually, it's not really a spay, right? They're not actually removing anything . . . er . . . important." His palms sweated with the thought of surgical procedures, especially the ones that involved the loss of critical body parts.

It wasn't the first time I'd let my beliefs get in the way of a relationship. Any male carnivore ran in the other direction, afraid, no doubt, of tofu recipes or stories of my brief internship in the dairy industry. Before vet school, I spent a summer with a bovine veterinarian, helping to treat wounds in dairy cows. Because they were overcrowded, stressed and living on concrete, the cows often developed abscesses from rubbing against the barn walls. My morning job was to gently flush pus out of the draining abscesses and, in the afternoon, give hormone injections as the meat truck arrived, picking up the older cows that could no longer keep up with the extremely high milk production requirements. It was a live commercial for the vegan diet. I dreamed at night about milk and pus, pus and milk, pretty soon confusing the two. From that point on, I had a knack for turning a nice summer date at the ice cream parlor into a recap of my short-term jaunt as an abscess cleaner— the reason I preferred sorbet.

Before I started dancing tango, I dated another young veterinarian, David, only to find out later that our Celtic passion would gradually be replaced by clashing Irish tempers. David was an artist with a deeply complex soul, full of unpredictable expectations and elaborate emotions. He exuded a sense of endless searching with a thirst that could never be quenched.

As we sat eating sorbet cones, looking dreamily at the sky, we watched a single blue balloon gently float upwards. I imagined a child had accidentally let it go. It was pretty, this balloon, and my eyes followed enviously, admiring its ability to rise above the heat of the city and all our earthly human dramas. David abruptly broke my daze. "Well, there goes another sea turtle." That was *his* date-ruining summer job, counting sea turtles and performing autopsies to report their cause of death.

"What do you mean?" I asked, watching the balloon disappear.

"When a balloon lands in the ocean, and its color fades, to a sea turtle it resembles a jellyfish. When the turtle consumes the plastic, it causes a foreign body obstruction." David was too much like me, too apt to trade in a sweet summer night for a piece of harsh reality.

Life never seemed as harsh as after my own surgery, lying there twitching, drooling and muttering on a steel table. I felt like a cold bag of soggy russet potatoes. I woke up from my procedure, second to last in a row of steel gurneys, with old people moaning on both sides and nurses gossiping from their nearby station. I considered the possibility that I had died. *So purgatory is filled with old groaning people.* The last time I had been around the elderly, they were considerate and quiet, and spoke with elegant British accents as they thanked me for trimming their thick toenails or serving them high tea and scones. There on the gurney, I quickly sat up to announce, "I have to pee!" It seemed like a normal response to the realization that life wasn't over. Thankful, I shuffled my way to a small adjacent bathroom.

I had to bargain with a nurse in order to be discharged early. It was too late to offer my firstborn, so I wondered if she'd settle for a bribe. Another moan emanated from the row of post-op patients. Within two or three minutes, I somehow succeeded in walking a straight line, concentrating so hard that it made my head hurt. Mind over matter. Right foot. Left foot. Right foot. "Wow, that was a record-speed recovery," the nurse said. Proud that I had fooled the nurse, I met Lorenzo in the waiting area. Without warning, I leaned over and vomited on his lap, marking the perfect end of our relationship.

After my surgery, I felt a dramatic sense of relief and happiness, two emotions I was unable to share with my friends or family members who still wished I would have children. Pleased to have followed my own heart, rather than live out the dreams of others, I would never doubt my decision. Now I could focus on caring for animals, without the distraction of creating another new life.

There was so much that I still needed to learn. There were classes on acupuncture, chiropractic and most numerous of them all, plant medicine.

Over the first few nights that followed my procedure, I tended to my three small incisions. I applied a thin layer of delicately infused Arnica oil, a powerful medicine to minimize swelling, hasten healing and reduce scarring. "You have to heal yourself before you can help others," I remembered Iris preaching from her plantain pulpit one day. "Doctors who smoke and eat junk food aren't practicing what they preach," she had said, looking up at me as she primped the blue satin petals of her poppies, "but you, now you'll be different. You'll fix yourself first." That night, I fell into a peaceful slumber, dreaming about Arnica, a cheery yellow flower arising from heart-shaped leaves.

The Terrier with Attitude

A COLD WET NOSE woke me the day after my procedure. As I groggily opened my eyes, I saw a scurry of a dog shadow, like a slick black sea lion, popping up from an ocean of blankets. One by one, Smudge brought me a parade of toys, her generous offering of alms. Once she surmised I was not interested, she grabbed her favorites, gripping them between her jaws and dropping them delicately on my head: a fuzzy snowman, a Tyrannosaurus head, a green caterpillar and an octopus's left tentacle.

I tried to laugh at the array of misfit toys, but that hurt my abdomen, so instead, I just held Smudge close, rubbing her belly. It was the same belly I'd rubbed for twelve years. I could not imagine that one day I'd be forced to find joy without her. Would that even be possible? "Smudge, if anything ever happens to you, I'm locking myself in a closet for a week." She blinked and wriggled her nose into the crook of my elbow.

Her idea of herself was inflated even before I bolstered it. Weighing only twenty pounds, she confidently pranced up to large dogs, even ones with battle scars and tattered ears. With her tail held high, she growled as she leaped from side to side, attempting to challenge them to a race. Smudge was an adventurer, preferring a mountain hike in the snow over a sniff-trip around the block. She feared nothing and confronted everything.

I picked Smudge from a handful of practice surgery dogs. It was the autumn of 1992, in Pullman, Washington, and I was in my third year of veterinary school. I sat just outside junior surgery studying the numerous types of suture knots. "Don't open that cage!" exclaimed the surgery technician. But before she could finish her sentence, I had already opened it and a black streak shot out from the chain-link enclosure. "She's liable to squirt everywhere!" the tech warned. We both chased after the small bolt of lightning throughout the hallways of junior surgery. The technician had been frustrated with the little dog and I could see why. Bolstered by fear and speed, the terrier escaped us at every turn.

As if she were the star in a freak show, the pint-sized black terrier screamed and bolted towards me. She suddenly stopped with a crazy glare, crouched low to the ground and slowly crawled towards me across the cement floor. Upon reaching my shoe, she immediately flipped over on her back exposing her new crooked spay incision. Before I could move, a moat of yellow liquid quickly surrounded both of us. Oblivious to the fact that her whole backside was saturated with urine, she stared up at me, her body motionless, her eyes wide with fear. I looked at the technician as I shook the urine off my foot. "Is this how she charms people?"

"Well, she's charmed her way back to the shelter. That truck is waiting outside to take her back, along with all the other dogs no one adopted." The technician pointed out the window towards the parking lot and then towards a row of larger dogs. "Why don't you take one of these?" Most were black Labradors slated for non-survival practice surgeries, their thick tails gently drumming against the walls of the steel cages. I tried to avert my eyes because their plight hurt me too. When deciding between conventional surgery class which resulted in euthanizing healthy animals after practice surgeries and alternative surgery class, there was no contest for me. I had opted for the alternative, learning on cadavers that had died from natural causes. I looked over at the dogs' longing eyes, eyes between bars, the eyes of the unwanted. The technician interrupted my thoughts. "That little black dog is a real nut. We had to move her twice because she made the rest of them nervous." As my colleague guided me away from the neurotic terrier, I couldn't help but gravitate back towards her as she lay completely still, upside down in a puddle of urine.

In that moment, I reacted as I have through much of my life, from my gut instead of my brain. Some impulsive decisions I'd later regret, while others I'd cherish. This one I would label as one of my proudest, when ignoring perfectly good advice came out even better than okay. I said, "Perfect. I'll take her." My decision was met with a roll of the technician's eyes. I signed an adoption form, copying the number from the dog's metal tag before removing it: *36541. Small black terrier mutt. Donna Kelleher, junior.* And then I asked for a towel.

Motionless on her back, the small dog blankly stared at me. I wrapped her up in the towel like a burrito, lifted her from the floor into a sink and rinsed her off. I replaced her metal tag with a rope leash and carried her out the door. The little terrier then took her first deep breath of freedom in months.

Instead of obediently trotting beside me, she lunged back and forth at the end of the leash, rubber-band-like, as we glanced through windows at the wondrous images of vet school: a three-legged dog with his IV still in place, a one-eyed orange cat in an oxygen chamber, an Arabian mare with a cast up to her elbow. These were all sights I had ignored during the last three years, but the terrier's surge of energy helped me look at them with new eyes.

When we got home, I studied her closely. Looking like a miniature black Labrador, she ran as fast as any big dog. She was an uncontrolled, frenzied splash of energy. But her most defining characteristic was her ears, disproportionately large for her head and folding inwards, halfway through their length.

Every time she caught my eye, she came dutifully, tipped upside down and peed beside me as though her urine was a gift of submission. Discipline would make it worse. I was no dog trainer, but I figured that out. I'd wrap her in another towel and patiently march her off to the sink again. Her behavior problems were too numerous to count, and she unabashedly laid them out for public scrutiny. I only wished that everyone, including myself, could be more like her, more truly authentic, not just because the world would be better for it, but because it would be more honest, more pure, more dog.

Turning my new dog over, I inspected her jagged spay incision. I recalled my first spay surgery and how difficult it was to keep the scalpel straight when I was shaking so much with the worry of excess bleeding. "Incisions heal from side to side," my surgery professor reassured me, noting my excessively long incision. I overheard one of the other students quietly mutter, "Well, that's a good thing." I examined my patient a week later, thrilled to see she had healed completely; her recovery gave me faith in the innate healing abilities of my patients.

Maybe this neurotic terrier could be my mascot, I thought, picturing her at the door of my future shiny veterinary clinic, greeting clients and welcoming their pets. I thought of the less-than-perfect mascots I'd seen at other clinics: an incontinent Jack Russell terrier, a grey tabby who needed his bladder squeezed twice a day but otherwise seemed happy enough, a yellow Labrador given up for intestinal problems and a penchant for chewing shoes. Now all I needed was a name for my new friend. It's considered bad luck to name a clinic animal Lucky, so that one was out. I looked down at a note card on the floor, the most recent object she had peed on. The ink had smudged and I could no longer read the words. "That's it! Smudge!"

Once Smudge became accustomed to the strange notion of a leash and collar, we walked. And walked. And ran. All over Pullman we would go, for miles in each direction, across fields and up to Kamiak Butte, a rare patch of sparse forest overlooking miles of treeless rolling hills. "See, Smudge, those are wheat fields." We sat together looking west at the pink sunset on waves of straw tones. Wherever I pointed, her eyes followed and her tail wagged.

Behind her eyes, I knew there was a dog that understood me, even at times when I did not understand myself. Smudge had a habit of hinting at the truth, even if it hurt. If I spent too much time watching television or talking on the phone, she made me aware that I was missing out on life. Her messages were always crystal clear. I looked at the rich, brown earth color of her irises and into the black of her pupils to a soul that was not unlike mine. When she wrinkled her forehead or twitched the whiskers above her eyes even slightly, her whole expression changed, communicating fear, apprehension, curiosity, sadness, elation, and most of all, love. In neurology class, I learned that her brain's limbic or emotional center was the same size proportionally as mine.

Smudge became my study subject, along with thick veterinary textbooks piled on either side of me, each one heavier than two Smudges. I stretched her out on my lap, held her mouth open between my middle finger and forefinger and inspected the wear of her dental cusps, the best way to assess a fully grown dog's age. "I don't know, Smudge, you might be two years old." She'd wag no matter how old I'd proclaim her to be. I studied the crevasses of her ears, and peered at the back of her green iridescent retina with an ophthalmoscope. I practiced my cranial nerve exam, brushing each side of Smudge's face with a cotton ball held by a pair of hemostats; by shining a penlight into each eye while I covered the other one, I could evaluate her pupillary light reflex and the third cranial nerve. She loved the attention, but when visitors came by, she'd retreat to a nearby closet, one of the many spaces preventatively lined with cellophane wrap.

When I came home each day, she'd leap up like a flea and spray urine in every direction, all over the kitchen, the stove, and especially me. Although I had become accustomed to the odd behavior, considering it more of a nuisance than a frustration, the presence of visitors compounded the problem, often doubling the urine output. When guests would arrive, I commonly spent the first several minutes on my knees, soaking up urine with reams of towels. Rather than the red carpet treatment, Smudge and I presented our visitors with a blotchy yellow throw rug.

To complicate matters, Smudge broke with a bout of kennel cough, hacking throughout the night. I knew that, within a few weeks, she would improve on her own, but my neighbor suggested that I return Smudge and get a registered puppy with a pedigree I could depend on. "A nice standard poodle," he said. I had already learned in internal medicine classes that a large percentage of diseases affected primarily purebred dogs and cats. And my mixed breed mutt was more likely to be free from a growing list of congenital and chronic medical problems.

I had no interest in discarding "the Smudge." If I returned her to the shelter, I might have less mess and more time, but I knew I would miss her terribly. I would reflect upon what I lost, left with the nagging fact that, were the tables turned, she would never have given up on *me*. Instead of sending her back, I tried calming music, flower essences and a new, patented, calm-your-dog-down tee shirt with a picture of a serene crescent moon on her chest. Unfortunately, with her front legs threaded through the shirt, Smudge appeared unable to move, frozen in place, as if the shirt were a canine straitjacket. It seemed that nothing short of heavy pharmaceuticals would relieve her anxiety.

After a few more weeks, I came up with a new idea. I left a container of dog treats just outside the front door, ready for use whenever I returned to the house. While holding a treat in one hand, I would carefully open the door with the other, slowly presenting Smudge with the cookie, before she had time to urinate. My neighbor shook his head at me from the walkway between our houses. Ignoring him, I peered down to see Smudge's reaction. She took the treat and ran into a corner to eat it. It worked! It was the first time since I'd adopted her that I did not have to spend an hour cleaning when I got home. With this clever distraction, Smudge never returned to her leaky old ways.

Even with her submissive urination resolved, Smudge still demonstrated many neurotic behaviors. When I trimmed my own fingernails, Smudge would run under the couch to hide for hours, with only her black tail protruding, shaking at the thought that I might then trim hers. And while driving to the mountains for hiking or backpacking trips, Smudge would whine and screech incessantly with excitement. Even with a blindfold to cover her eyes, and ear plugs to save my hearing, Smudge turned a relaxing nature experience into a symphony of anticipatory screaming, at least until she sprang from the car. The behavior drove me crazy and lasted most of her nineteen years on this planet, but it did serve to screen out potential boyfriends. Men patient enough to handle Smudge's shrieks stayed for a while. Others were eliminated with one simple hike.

Unlike a Labrador, who often has trouble deciding between a ball and food, Smudge knew what she wanted, and that was to be with me. A time would come, a few years later, when Smudge would grow so confident that she became my demonstration dog, helping me teach continuing education classes all over Seattle. If I talked about chiropractic treatments, I'd stretch her spine on the podium to show the location of each unique vertebra. If acupuncture was our focus, I would run my finger along the sides of her body mimicking the pathway of chi in the acupuncture meridians. During lectures on herbal medicine, I poured hot water over leaves and passed the concoction to the audience while Smudge leaped at a chance to try it.

Our favorite act was fondly titled, "Yes, You Can Brush Your Dog's Teeth, Too." I stood in front of a wide-eyed group of animal welfare enthusiasts, holding up a new purple toothbrush and called out, "Smudge, let's brush our teeth!" The little dog ran between chairs and leaped onto the stage, excited to get a special treat after complying with the toothbrush. The larger the crowd, the better she performed. In front of one hundred open-jawed onlookers, she tilted her head amiably with each stroke of the toothbrush. First right side, then left, repeating the sequence for the bottom set. Her grand finale consisted of a tail wag, bark and rollover, all for a tiny liver treat. Smudge always knew how to steal the show, and my heart.

A Need for Acceptance

IT HAD BEEN a year since I graduated from veterinary school. Smudge, Sampson and I moved to the Midwest, pursuing what I thought was the career of my dreams. But my time in Chicago was difficult, largely because I worried that I had spent almost a decade studying for a profession that increasingly did not seem to suit me. I found comfort in the memory of Iris's delicate heirloom roses and the round raindrops that sparkled on their petals like diamonds.

One quiet Sunday morning, I sat on a small beach on Lake Michigan in Wilmette, Illinois, as the dogs frolicked in the sand. Across the street was the Bahá'í temple, a three-tiered white circular structure with ornate latticework. As the dogs played with sticks at the lake's edge, I read the temple's pamphlet aloud.

"The Bahá'í's core belief is in oneness of humankind," I reported, wondering about *dog* kind. Sampson gazed at me, waiting for more. "It originated in Iran. The Bahá'ís practice daily prayer, and avoid excessive materialism, partisan politics, backbiting, alcohol, drugs and gambling." The dogs grew bored. Smudge stole a stick from Sampson who gladly gave it up, content just to be with us. Smudge had reached the height of her terrierness, exerting dominance whenever she could, but Sampson's easygoing ways increased with each passing year. I continued on. "Their core beliefs also include fellowship with followers of all religions, a life dedicated to the service of humanity and the independent investigation of truth. Sermons are prohibited and only scriptural texts are read. They worship god without denominational restrictions." I took a moment to reflect on such a philosophy.

Back then, if I needed an antidote to sadness, I would think of the sweet silky aroma of Iris's rosebush. But when looking for an antidote to feeling lost in my own career, I could only think of my mother's steadfast dedication to hers. Like the Bahá'í, she was able to embrace many different belief systems, thriving on cultural diversity and unencumbered by any professional or philosophical restrictions. On the contrary, I felt confined by medical and moral paradigms about which I felt more skeptical with each passing year.

After graduating from veterinary school, I began work at

45

a typical veterinary hospital. But within a few weeks, I knew there was a problem. I just didn't fit the mold of conventional veterinarian. Most of my moral dilemmas centered around animal welfare, nutritional philosophy and pharmaceutical treatments. Problems arose when my ideals conflicted with what might be considered routine veterinary procedures. In essence, there was my refusal to perform the procedure and the inevitable result. The procedure: Euthanasia for an otherwise healthy cat due to clawing the owner's face. The result: A new feline roommate for Smudge. The procedure: Painful dewclaw removal for a litter of two-day-old puppies. The result: A stern reprimand from the practice owner. The procedure: Euthanasia of a white boxer puppy delivered by Caesarian section. The result: The loss of another job.

I called my mom to ask her opinion about my plight. "Donna, make it quick. I'm boarding a plane to Namibia," she said. So, instead I just complained to my dogs. Smudge understood. It wasn't that I felt righteous; I just wanted to avoid that looming sense of guilt that I felt when I compromised my principles. As much as I wanted to be an amiable poodle, like Sampson, I was, in reality, a headstrong terrier. And although neither Smudge nor I wanted to be contrary, that is exactly what people decided we were. Less than a year out of vet school and I had already worked in twelve different veterinary clinics. In a few of them, I just filled in for a few days. These I preferred; by the time I wore out my welcome, my shift had ended.

Despite four years in veterinary school, my mind often veered away from my conventional medical training. In Western medicine, if the diagnosis was an infection, the treatment would be antibiotics. For me, even this simple scenario was fraught with questions: What about the patient's immune system? Why was he so susceptible to the infection? I viewed the body as a fortress and the immune system as its army, which could be potentially weakened by genetics, malnutrition, over-vaccination, extreme emotions and adrenal suppression. As I considered these questions, I realized I was more interested in addressing the underlying cause of disease than merely treating the superficial symptoms. But I had chosen a profession that seemed to be more interested in erasing those pesky symptoms than in addressing anything deeper.

I looked up at the sky and became transfixed by the acrobatics of seagulls that seemed happy even though they were far away from any sea. They soared through the air without crabs to fight over or seaweed to sift through. Below them, wind pushed ripples on the horizon. The dogs and I gazed out at the expanse of the lake. My eyes searched for an island, a ship or anything to break up the monotony. With nothing visible on the surface, the lake appeared completely uniform, every water molecule interconnected to form a seamless whole. I closed my eyes to feel the energy of the waves passing through my own body, knowing that all mammals are made primarily of water.

The sun glanced at us from between the clouds and I watched Sampson soaking up its rays. Even when he was young, he always seemed perfect in temperament and sensibilities, rarely barking or raising a fuss of any kind. He knew when I needed comforting or when I needed space. Sampson was everyone's favorite dog. His personality mirrored a quiet mountain lake with its glass-like serenity. On the contrary, Smudge's disposition expanded and receded, as forceful and unstoppable as the ocean's tides, and often with a fierce undercurrent. Smudge growled at a rock on the beach for no good reason while Sampson just wanted to sit on my lap.

Much of my childhood revolved around my mother's job as an international studies professor. Even before I attended high school, Mom had studied and lived in many countries all over the world, opening our door to the world's people. All of our international guests were conflict solvers, inventors of innovative solutions in their own communities. With courses on achieving peace as her specialty, Mom was most alive on a plane, headed to the site of a previous conflict.

Due to her open-mindedness, my mother tried not to force religious belief upon us, even though church was an important part of her early life. As if we were her students, she taught Neil and me to view the world and the actions of mankind through a microscope of analysis, explaining that the actions of the world's people, including our fellow Americans, were based on an interaction between their own religious beliefs, cultural values and systematic propaganda. There were never only two sides of a story. Mom viewed society as a Rubik's cube, multifaceted with a complicated pattern of reason. By example, she had raised two scientists, two souls on opposite trajectories.

"There is no such thing as Santa Claus. It's a lie parents tell to their children," she said, matter-of-factly, one year as we watched *Rudolph*. I was crushed. But even at eight years old, the thought of some fat guy dressed in red and squeezing down our chimney seemed a little far-fetched. Besides, once Santa discovered that the hearth was Tigger's back-up litter box, the gift-giving would have ended.

My childhood pressures were nothing compared to the images in the magazines Mom left on our kitchen table. When no one was looking, I studied the faces of people affected by war, poverty and starvation. Images of suffering children from the Middle East, Africa and Central America stayed frozen in my mind. But the photographs of rural Nicaraguan kids, victims of President Reagan's well-funded Contra revolution, struck me the most. Worse than the bloodstains was the desperate way that their fearful eyes clung to the camera, grasping for anything beyond their world. A term my mother threw around, *human rights violation,* did little to console me. My mother wanted me to be as tough as her, but I was too sensitive for my own good. Still, she did not hide the world from me.

But I hid from it. I hid under my long hair or, when that wasn't good enough, under a crocheted blue poncho. My thoughts would spin around me, eventually running out of steam and stalling into acceptance. I occasionally saw a white snout make its way into my blue healing cocoon and I would realize that Sampson had pushed his way under my poncho, through my thick hair and into my private healing space. Whiskers brushed against my nose, eventually luring me out to see a lovely sunset. And his empty bowl.

Later, during my teenage years, my mom sponsored a series of international guests. Some had never left their remote villages before coming to America. They came from Africa, South America and Northern Ireland, among other countries. But the one I remember most was a man named Tham from northeast Thailand. At night, he found peace as he played his *sueng*, a type of lute, in our living room. He emanated a contemplative kindness that I had scarcely seen before. Even Sampson sat up to enjoy his melodies.

Tham started a project in the northern and eastern villages of Thailand to give girls valuable training in handicrafts, basic literacy and math, preparing them for careers as shopkeepers so they would be financially useful to their families. In that way, parents might think twice about selling their daughters to the sex tourism trade in Phuket. I reeled when I learned about the ordeal of these girls' lives, most of whom were about my age.

On the third day of his stay, Tham finally said, "Where are the villages?" But what he meant was, *Where are all the people?* I imagined his heart breaking when he saw the state of suburban America, a country seemingly in lockdown, as people sat glued to their televisions. He was used to his world in rural Thailand, where villagers spent much of the day socializing in tight communities. Tham was the first bona fide vegan I ever met, though he knew nothing about that label. In preparation for his visit, we went looking for soymilk, which took us hours to find, and when we did find it, he drank it just to be polite. But what he really enjoyed was his own Thai tea, *cha wan*, which he had brought from home. He would stand at our cluttered kitchen counter and sprinkle the naturally sweet black tea with dried rose petals, smiling warmly as he inhaled the steam.

Remembering Tham, I slowly gathered our things from the beach: a purple leash, a Frisbee and a collapsible water dish. The dogs and I crossed the road to the Bahá'í temple garden to investigate its grand roses, richly colored with plum red, salmon pink and butter yellow. I thought of how protective Iris had been of her rosebush. She'd let me tend to anything in her garden, but the rose was off-limits. I had always assumed she did not trust me to shape it to her expectations, but as the years passed, I later surmised that she just wanted to spend as much time absorbing its beauty as possible. Sipping on some peppermint iced tea, she once said, "Rose oil opens the tightest of hearts." As roses go, hers were not much to look at, single layered with a center of orange surrounded by dull yellow petals. But their sweet scent filled the nostrils, spicy as cardamom, smooth as satin and sweet as honeysuckle, nature's guaranteed antidote for depression.

Despite my own career dilemmas, I felt peace spread within me as I stood in front of the temple with its great lacy pillars and circular roof mingling with the sky. Gazing at each of its nine sun-filled domes that seemed to move with the passing clouds, in the spirit of the Bahá'í faith, I realized it was okay that I was different. Just as my mother's career had blossomed through the exploration of diversity, mine would feature a holistic niche within the confines of the conventional medical world. I sunk my nose into the center of a yellow rose and filled my lungs with its sweetness.

One Day in a Veterinarian's Life

MY CLINIC in north Seattle is not a typical veterinary hospital. I have neither street signs nor a shingle above my door. But over the years, my practice has grown nonetheless, mainly through word of mouth. Clients find my name at dog parks, holistic pet stores or even through their hairdressers. I see a parade of old dogs: Labradors, pit bulls, Rottweilers, shepherds, and everything in between. But a few things unite them all—grey muzzles and stiff, creaky bodies. Their diseases are often chronic and vary widely, usually involving aging joints, achy spines or stressed neurologic systems. Whatever the problem, my job is to keep my patients comfortable enough to walk, trot or even run again. I strive to find treatments using minimal or no pharmaceuticals that allow these animals to renew their old activities: running after squirrels, chasing their own tails and harassing the family cat.

Mac, an aging sheepdog, hadn't chased the pesky family cat in months. He had started to become stiff and weak around age eleven. After his caretaker, Linda, had tried giving him anti-inflammatory medications, which caused multiple side effects, she then decided to try acupuncture. A nurse at a busy inner-city emergency hospital, Linda was delighted when Mac's symptoms improved after just three sessions of chiropractic adjustments and electroacupuncture.

Linda told me that, in his younger years, Mac had cost her thousands in veterinary bills due to his unfortunate habit of tracking down and cornering the local porcupines. Each pointed encounter resulted with Mac in the veterinary hospital waiting room, a crowd gathering to see his snout packed with white glistening quills poking up through his shaggy grey hair. Other pet owners asked Linda if this was Mac's first encounter with a porcupine. She would then have to admit that Mac lived for the moment, apparently forgetting the painful results of his previous encounters.

As much as Linda hated Mac's hobby, she now wished that he could find the energy to resume the activities of his youth. "If only he would take interest in chasing things again," Linda said, hoping that he might downgrade to some safer form of prey, like squirrels or chipmunks. Although Mac began to feel much better, an unfortunate collision with the front door left him stiff again. I suspected that his poor eyesight and lack of depth perception might have caused the accident, but Linda blamed the next-door neighbor's cat that often taunted Mac through the window.

Whatever the reason, Mac hobbled into my office early one Monday morning, limping again on his right front and left rear. This is the point when some people would have suggested euthanasia, but Linda had no interest in giving up on her canine companion. So my role was to relieve his pain and get his legs under him again. Linda looked at me. "He's still getting around okay and his appetite is good, especially after walks to the mailbox. When he gives up, we'll know it." Linda also knew that waxing and waning symptoms could often be part of the body's normal healing process.

Gently, I threaded each needle into acupuncture points around Mac's shoulders, hips and back, each point releasing enkephalins and other natural pain-relieving compounds. After a minute or two, Mac eased down for a nap, relaxing with the treatment and the instant pain relief it gave him. If I could give Mac, a dog who had lived life to the fullest, even a little reprieve from his symptoms, then my day was worthwhile. Linda smiled and thanked me as they both headed out the door.

Mac's treatment was finished but my day was just getting started. After saying goodbye to Mac and Linda, I greeted a middle-aged couple in the waiting room. The woman was gently petting a quiet puppy in her lap while her husband stood next to her, looking as though he felt out of place. He seemed uninterested in my collection of books about feline massage and raw diets.

Transitions like these were not always easy; one moment, I was gently supporting a weak elderly patient, and the next, I was seeing a young puppy with his whole life to live. But on days like this, that's just what my job entailed. This particular puppy was a fourteen-week-old oversized Australian shepherd named Nelson. He was grey and brindled with ears that stood up even when the rest of him couldn't. For the past month, Nelson had become progressively weaker. His caretakers had taken him to a neurology specialist where both an MRI and CAT scan had failed to reveal the cause of his symptoms. I knelt down on the floor to examine him. His neurologic reflexes in the hind limbs were extremely weak. But even more troubling to me was the way he appeared to give up, falling back on his hind end. With a resigned gaze, he looked up at all of us for help. I was concerned that his hind leg weakness was rapidly deteriorating into a generalized paralysis, as his symptoms had begun spreading to the front legs too.

"Doctor Smith thought you might be able to help Nelson," the woman said, her hands never leaving the puppy. This was the first time a neurologist had ever referred a case to me. It was usually the other way around. By referring Nelson to my care, Dr. Smith demonstrated an open-mindedness towards holistic modalities, a view that was uncommon back then in the veterinary profession.

A year earlier, I had called an internal medicine specialist to provide an update on a mutual patient. "Hello, Dr. Kittle? This is Dr. Donna Kelleher at Veterinary Holistic Clinic of Seattle. I am calling to tell you the good news that Fifi Johnson is doing well. I've discontinued her medications and prescribed a treatment regime of acupuncture and herbal medicine, but I hope that when she needs conventional care, Mrs. Johnson can still call you." The phone went silent. Then, my heart sank at the sound of a dial tone. Remembering this interaction, I felt even more grateful for Dr. Smith's faith in my healing abilities.

I read the detailed neurology report and the handwritten presumed diagnosis of progressive neuralgia, unknown etiology. Nelson's prognosis was listed as guarded, which essentially meant that given his rapid growth rate, if this puppy did not start to improve very soon, he would likely be euthanized. I looked at the puppy and sighed. A few moments of silence passed. "How long has Nelson been afflicted with these symptoms? Have they always been there?" I asked. The answers would give me a hint as to whether Nelson's symptoms were congenital or acquired.

"That's just it," the woman said. "He was normal until he was about eight weeks old. He started wobbling in his back legs about a month ago. That's why we can't figure it out." Her husband hovered on the other side of the exam room, folding his arms in front of him, while his wife stayed attentive to her puppy.

Because there was no history of flea medications or other neurotoxins, two possible causes came to mind: either Nelson had a rare congenital disease, maybe a problem with the development of his spinal nerves, or he was reacting to a vaccine. Since I could do little about a congenital problem, my goal was to treat the potential vaccine reaction. No matter the cause, I needed to find treatments that could support and regenerate the nervous system.

As I puzzled over Nelson's treatment, I recalled the first miracle of healing I ever experienced. When I was five years old, my grandmother and I found a bumblebee flailing and struggling for life on the floor of our apartment. There was a golden hue to the sunlight that summer morning, and my grandmother placed a small drop of honey in front of the bee, which I thought had already died. Within a second after ingesting the honey, the bee miraculously flew out the window. It was such a small thing, this revival of a bumblebee, and yet it remained a special memory to me. Sometimes big problems have easy solutions.

I said, "It will be a team effort. Let's see what we can do for him."

"Do you think it will work? I mean, my husband wonders how

effective acupuncture really is." The woman looked embarrassed to admit that neither of them knew a thing about holistic medicine. But I knew that animals weren't aware that they were supposed to feel better after their treatment. Thus, they were free from the often-debated placebo effect.

"I don't mind if a client questions my therapies," I said. "It's natural for it to seem foreign." I chose three small packages of sterile hair-thin acupuncture needles, arranging them on the table in front of me. "Acupuncture works very well for a variety of neurological problems. However, the myelin sheath that surrounds and protects the spinal cord must be intact. So, if his symptoms are due to a demyelinating disease, it won't work." I looked at both of them. "But it won't be harmful either."

The first part of my approach was to strengthen the deficiency that may have been caused by the vaccinations. I prescribed a safe homeopathic treatment called *Thuja occidentalis*, made from the cedar tree, and instructed the couple on how to administer the remedy at home. I wrote down a list of suggestions, including a homemade diet with foods rich in carotenoids and nerve-enriching B vitamins. I also showed them how to prepare an herbal tea with nervine properties, capable of simultaneously relaxing and strengthening the nervous system.

Over the following month, the husband took charge of Nelson's physical therapy, gently stretching each limb in a passive range of motion. Each week, we met for an acupuncture treatment and I'd occasionally alter the herbal formula based on Nelson's symptoms. The original tea consisted of lion's mane mushroom, *Hericium erinaceus*; skullcap, *Scutellaria lateriflora*; and St. John's wort, *Hypericum perforatum*. As I formulated the combination of herbs, I studied each one closely, especially the lion's mane mushroom, a clump of tufted material that looked more like a meshwork of dense cotton than a mushroom. It reminded me of the "Doctrine of Signatures," an ancient, and largely unsubstantiated, philosophy stating that the herb resembles whichever body tissue it can heal. For lion's mane mushroom, which has been proven to regenerate nerve tissue, the doctrine seemed true: the loamy white mushroom closely resembles nervous system tissue, especially the brain's white matter.

As if he understood our healing motive, Nelson sat as motionless as possible, uncommon for a puppy, as I threaded tiny needles into association points along both sides of his vertebrae, and opened the *Du Mai*, an acupuncture meridian, down the center of his spine, using points located on the outside of the front and back feet. Every week, I repeated the electroacupuncture treatments, moving my points to the areas with the most severe pathology. Slowly, the puppy regained use of his back legs, first kicking them out erratically and then walking, wobbling from right to left.

With each small progression, we celebrated and then moved

on, careful not to consider him cured too early. "Don't count your chickens . . ." Iris had always warned. Her superstition about gloating sunk into my consciousness. "Humility is just as important to healers as good medicine," she used to say.

Nelson made a complete and permanent recovery over the next eight weeks. As he bounded out the door after his last appointment, I hoped the momentum of his successful healing might carry over to my next patient, a golden retriever named Jasper. I imagined it would look like osmosis, an abstract cellular concept I puzzled over in biochemistry class in which electrolytes and fluids could pass through cell membranes, creating a current of ionic flow. I felt myself riding a wave of therapeutic success.

Challenging Cases

BUT EVERY WAVE must break.

When she was fourteen, Smudge was struck with mast cell cancer of the highest malignancy. I gasped when I found the red, rapidly growing tumor on the inside of her thigh, along the liver meridian. In the ideal world, the mass needed to be excised, but due to Smudge's advanced age and her elevated liver enzymes, I worried about her ability to withstand general anesthesia.

Although I would have liked to calmly ask my fellow veterinarian, Jeff Blake, to remove the mass with just a local anesthetic, I instead shrieked, terrier-like, over the phone at him, practically hyperventilating, "Smudge and I are on our way!" Jeff worked at a large veterinary hospital in north Seattle, and many of his coworkers could not understand why I was not willing to remove the tumor myself. But Jeff understood. As veterinarians, it was difficult to stay objective when treating our own animals. So Smudge and I waited until all the clients had gone and the three of us were alone. A few hospitalized cats were the only witnesses to our first mini argument.

"Can you remove it without using general anesthesia?" I asked him. He was on his best behavior then as we had not yet started dating. I urged Jeff to perform the surgery because I trusted him as well as his expertise. His skills surpassed those of most veterinarians I knew. And besides, I could barely tolerate Smudge's reaction to the much simpler procedure of trimming her toenails. My request rubbed against the organized grain of Jeff's persona. He did everything according to the book, removing mast cell tumors using general anesthesia and obtaining wide surgical margins. Veterinarians generally preferred to remove as much of the local tissue as possible in an effort to prevent the tumor from growing back again.

"Please," I begged him pathetically. "It would take her days to bounce back from anesthesia. She is so old. And the tumor is small enough to remove with a local." I flipped Smudge on her back to show him the red, swollen and inflamed thumbnail of a thing, which we assumed to be malignant based on its appearance. "My herbs should prevent it from coming back," I added, feeling guilty that I hadn't already started to give Smudge cancer-prevention herbs or supplements.

Removing much of the surrounding tissue made sense, but I knew this was most likely a mast cell tumor, a blood-borne cancer with cells that could rapidly spread throughout the area. I had faith in Jeff's skills and he had faith in mine. For years he had heard stories of Iris and all my herbal teachers, listening patiently as I described restoring health to my patients. "They pretty much heal themselves," I said, smiling because I knew how much he believed, as I did, in the wisdom of a universal healing force. He had seen thousands of animals heal with only minimal medications, fluid therapy or no treatment at all.

Smudge looked up at him, sizing up his commitment until eventually Jeff compromised his by-the-book scruples. I held off the vein running down Smudge's front leg and Jeff injected a sedative. Gently, he clipped the fur around the small tumor as I held Smudge upside down on her back. Using a small needle, he slowly injected the local anesthetic. After waiting a few minutes for it to take effect, he deftly excised the small mass with a scalpel blade, leaving four neat sutures where the tumor had been.

With the lump removed, I began treating the constitutional weakness that had allowed Smudge's cancer to grow in the first place. Even though her blood work revealed no anemia, there was a pale quality to her tongue, indicative of blood deficiency. Smudge had previously been on a diet consisting of equal volumes of chicken, quinoa and ground vegetables, but now, given her current illness, I eliminated the grain portion of her diet and fed her strictly meat and vegetables. The drive-through bank tellers, who insisted on showering her with wheat-based cookies, were disappointed. "No thanks, we're cancer survivors," I said, leaving them stumped as to why I would make such a statement. Ground turkey thigh meat, along with organic organ meats and ground raw dark vegetables, would help enrich her blood. I also mixed red reishi and other immune-modulating mushrooms into her food. But the most important change was the addition of specific Chinese herbs and nettle leaf powder to restore health to her liver and blood. While treating Smudge's blood deficiency at home, Jasper came to see me at the clinic. He also had been afflicted with cancer, but his was caused by nearly the opposite energetic disturbance.

I met Jasper at the door of my office. He dragged himself in, the toenails of each of his four paws scraping the floor as though he barely had the strength to hold his head up. At ten years old, illness had stolen his youthful fire and harnessed his bouncy personality. His caretakers, Wendy and Greg, slowly walked in with their dog. They felt sick themselves, having just received Jasper's diagnosis from the veterinary specialty clinic.

I looked at the results of his ultrasound, trying not to reveal the gravity of his situation in my expression. Liver tumors. There were two of them, eight and ten centimeters in diameter, about half as large as a liver lobe itself. Though we wished the diagnosis were incorrect, Jasper wore the grim news in his uncharacteristically sluggish demeanor.

A slight reduction in Jasper's appetite had brought his owners to their conventional veterinarian. Wendy and Greg had hoped that Jasper was suffering from a simple infection, curable with a seven-day course of antibiotics. But then they noticed something different about his eyes. "One of our only clues was his uveitis," Wendy said. Greg nodded as the couple recounted Jasper's recent history. The Millers had noticed that Jasper's eyes were redder than usual, a bloodshot ring on the outside of the white sclera. The ophthalmologist ran a blood panel and found Jasper's liver enzymes to be hundreds of times their normal levels. According to the principles of Chinese medicine, the health of the liver can be seen through the eyes. But now, with Jasper's increasing weakness, his eye problems seemed insignificant.

After Wendy and Greg left the eye specialist's office, they consulted with two surgeons who both agreed that surgically removing Jasper's tumors would be too risky.

A biopsy of the tumors would also be dangerous due to his prolonged blood clotting times and propensity to bleed excessively. Chemotherapy might give him a few months, but without the biopsy, the oncologist could not formulate a treatment protocol or predict an outcome, least of all a favorable one. So, without surgery and chemotherapy, the Millers were left with no treatment options.

"Did your vet prescribe anything to help Jasper?" I asked, hoping that their veterinarian would at least offer vitamin injections.

"Just prednisone," Wendy answered. "I don't really call that supportive therapy." Her training as a nurse had helped her negotiate the tricky world of medical options.

"Eventually, there might be a place for low doses of corticosteroids, but I want to try some safer, more effective treatments first," I said. "Prednisone could have liver-damaging side effects, and it might increase his chances of infection."

When I first met Wendy and Greg, over seven years ago, Jasper was a bounding young dog with itchy skin and recurrent ear infections, early clues to his chronic liver imbalance. The couple sought solutions to these problems, but not pharmaceutical ones. They commuted over an hour and a half from their home in Port Orchard to my office in Seattle for our appointments. They emitted a quiet kindness, possibly because, with Jasper around, no one could get a word in edgewise. Jasper bounced off the walls, licking everyone in the room, while he panted and whined with excitement to see me.

"Jasper has responded very well to holistic treatments for his skin allergies," I said, pondering a new course of action. I looked down at Jasper's record and my medical notes from years ago. Often, dogs won't eat certain herbal formulas or ground raw vegetables mixed with their food, but Jasper had ingested the powdered, bitter-tasting herbal formulas and had responded quickly to herbs and acupuncture. With only four treatments, Jasper's allergy symptoms had completely disappeared.

Rather than lifting Jasper to the table and risking the rupture of his liver tumors, I knelt on the tile floor to examine him. He had always been a master of hiding his illness, but his tongue revealed the seriousness of his condition. Tongue diagnosis was a cornerstone of holistic medicine and as Jasper broke into a pant, we could see that his tongue was colored brick red, indicating severe stagnation and phlegm fire. The toxic heat had built up inside him, settling deep in his body tissues and simmering away his vital fluids.

"Is this our fault?" Greg asked. "Since he's an aging golden retriever, should we have known he'd get cancer and done something sooner to prevent it?"

"Of course not," I answered, explaining that genetics are only one possible cause for cancer. Over the years, I had seen so many dogs around ten years of age develop cancer, not only golden retrievers. "There are carcinogens everywhere, in our water, air and soil," I said. All too often, large chemical corporations governed the health of our environment and, by extension, our pets. I told the Millers to get rid of all their household cleaners and common weed-killing chemicals. Even lawn fertilizers that claimed to be safe were probably not. Glyphosate-containing lawn treatments had recently been linked to non-Hodgkin's lymphoma in humans. I imagined Jasper walking across a perfectly green, chemical-laden lawn with bare paws and then later unknowingly licking the chemicals from between his toes. At that moment, Iris's love for dandelions didn't seem so crazy.

"Also, I suggest Jasper not receive any more vaccinations," I added, stating that in 1999, veterinary adjuvants, the carrier component in many vaccines, were rated as moderately to highly carcinogenic by the World Health Organization. Many holistic practitioners believed that over-vaccination was responsible for genetic damage in purebred dogs. Vaccinations or their adjuvants may prevent certain genes from being expressed into protective proteins and enzymes as well as turning other genes on to produce unwanted or damaging proteins. Although routine vaccination protocols had been effective at preventing many infectious diseases, I suspected they might have played a role in Jasper's cancer.

Greg knelt down and Jasper licked his face. I continued, "Tumors are composed of a dog's own cells trapped in their early stage of rapid growth. The immune system should recognize and kill these cells. Possibly because of genetic or immune system weakness, these cells are allowed to proliferate out of control. These tumors were caused by a faulty wire in Jasper's own genes." I then told Wendy and Greg about Smudge's mast cell tumor. "It can happen to anyone," I said.

The first time I looked closely at malignant tumors, I worked in a necropsy lab, dissecting the small masses and placing them into formalin for histopathology. Our professor was a stickler, demanding accurate measurements on our necropsy reports, and nothing bothered him more than comparing tumors to fruit or vegetables. Still, I thought those little, dark red tumors looked just like pomegranate seeds, packed tightly against the stomach lining. They seemed so benign to me, maybe due to their small size. But Jasper's tumors were different. They were large and cumbersome and disrupted his hepatic circulation.

Wendy, Greg and I sat quietly in my office. The clock ticked loudly. A garbage truck drove by, reminding us of the world outside. We all fell silent for a while as we looked at Jasper, his back arched with abdominal discomfort. Even with the benefits of holistic medicine, I assumed that he had only days to live.

After several minutes, Wendy said, "I really want to try to save him." She lowered herself to the floor, instinctively cradling the dog's head. Greg grimaced with doubt. She continued, "I wish we could just cut those things out of there."

So did I. But I also realized that even if the surgeon was willing to excise the masses, removing them would not guarantee Jasper an extended life, as cells from those tumors may have already spread to other organs. "Even without surgery, there's always hope, Wendy," I said. And maybe by doing our best, we could give Jasper a little more quality time. I told the Millers that we could support Jasper's liver and immune system. Even if it was too late, if we made a real effort to help him, then when Jasper died, when his ashes were carried to their final resting place, we'd all look back to this day with clarity. At least we would have done our best to save him.

Deep inside, though, I still had my doubts. I was no stranger to difficult cases over the years. There had been many dogs and cats that I could not help, and those patients still haunted me.

As though sixteen years had rewound, I saw the grey-haired man wearing his pair of black-rimmed glasses, sitting in his wheelchair, his trusty German shepherd by his side. Though hundreds of clients had since come and gone, this old man and his dog still lingered in my memory. A perfect match, this man and dog, each dependent on the other, until the day they came to see me at a large, ten-doctor veterinary practice in Chicago. I could still hear the haunting guttural murmur of the man's oxygen tank as air flowed through his nasal tube, and his droning whisper, the only voice his lung condition afforded him. It seemed that his dog had developed a similar cough, and she, too, now heaved for air.

The man's son pulled me aside and said, "My dad and this dog are close, and if the dog dies, Dad dies," as if somehow this information would change my approach. But then, the son choked back tears and I realized he may have been holding on to the dim hope that this was only a bad case of pneumonia, something, anything with a treatment.

Unfortunately, radiographs revealed that the dog's lungs were full of cancer, with almost no remaining normal lung tissue. Now it was my job to deliver the bad news. I stopped with my hand on the exam room door, leaning into the knob, with the old man, his trusty dog and his son waiting on the other side. But I retreated into the bathroom instead. Wiping water around my eyes to mask my tears, I returned to the exam room with the devastating news. I thought to myself, *I'm not tough enough for this job.* These were the moments I never saw on a veterinary school brochure.

Back in Seattle, I was now a well-established holistic veterinarian, treating animals with arthritis, allergies, intervertebral disc disease and epilepsy. But I was still discovering the medical politics of cancer treatment. Most veterinarians considered herbal medicine solely as a way to alleviate side effects from the primary treatment of chemotherapy, radiation or surgery. It was my job not to reject the traditional cancer treatments, but to allow animal caregivers to make their own choices; in many cases those clients decided not to follow the path of conventional therapy. At that point, my treatments were no longer merely supportive, they were the only therapy left.

Using alternative medicine as primary therapy was met with a tremendous amount of skepticism from other veterinarians, who generally believed that these types of treatments were completely ineffective. Years earlier, I had treated and resolved a dog's osteosarcoma with a raw diet, herbal therapy, daily Reiki and immune-modulating mushrooms. We had a confirmed diagnosis including radiographs, a biopsy and a histopathology report. Yet the dog's regular veterinarian still dismissed the miraculous cure as coincidence. And although his final opinion was that the initial diagnosis had been wrong, he had been sufficiently convinced to offer amputation and chemotherapy.

People generally assume that there is just one acceptable way to treat cancer—with conventional medicine, chemotherapy, radiation, and surgery. Many oncologists today advocate not using any holistic medicine while a pet is under their care. They believe that herbal supplements and antioxidants are not well characterized and can have unforeseen and negative interactions with chemotherapy drugs. They also typically state that no special diets are necessary. While their approach may successfully treat some types of cancer, the risks can often outweigh the benefits, especially in older, compromised animals.

Contrary to their opinions, I believe that dietary therapy is critical in the treatment of cancer. For years, I used the energetics of food to treat many forms of disease. If a disease caused heat or inflammation, I'd prescribe organic, homemade, finely ground diets including cold-water fish, pork and green leafy vegetables to cool the inflammation. I might also prescribe raw diets which are cooling to the body. On the other hand, if a patient had a cold imbalance, his ears cool to the touch, I might prescribe cooked lamb or chicken, and warming vegetables like steamed rutabagas, turnips, parsnips and a tiny piece of fresh ginger. For either constitution, the introduction of live plant antioxidants, vitamins and minerals would be beneficial, especially since these ingredients are often unavailable in commercial diets. If herbs and homemade diets could help Jasper, I thought, why not try them?

"Donna, how long do you think he has?" Wendy asked as she slowly stroked her dog's ears, kneading them one after the other.

"Well," I said, brushing off the thought of malignancy, "at the very least, we can give him a good week."

"The other vets can't help him or they *won't*, I'm not sure which," she said, holding back tears. "We don't want chemotherapy but we *do* want treatment." Greg sat quietly, sadly resolved that he might have to say goodbye in a few short days.

Where would I find the resources to help Jasper? If I looked in my large veterinary books I would find very few treatment options aside from surgery and chemotherapy. At the time, books on holistic cancer therapy were essentially nonexistent.

I took a deep breath as I headed into my herbal pharmacy. Surrounded with dark amber jars of rich, fragrant dried leaves, roots and flowers, I searched for a quiet place within myself as if I were walking through a deep forest, far away from roads and people. Plant medicine, *my medicine*, had not let me down before. The plants had helped Smudge, but now I would be asking so much more of them: to heal Jasper from his severe phlegm fire cancer. To help him live even one week, we had to create a new state of balance in his body. I needed to choose herbs that could move energy, relieve heat and stimulate his sluggish immune system.

Stepping up on a stool to reach the jars and bottles of powdered herbs, I took down each bottle and grouped them into three formulas, reminding me of Iris's favorite three-pronged rake. The first would strengthen the body, bone marrow and immune system. I scooped equal portions of powdered ashwaganda and astragalas root. The next was a liver-strengthening formula. I combined nettle leaf, dandelion leaf, milk thistle and sweet Annie, each contributing its own special properties. The milk thistle would protect the remaining undamaged hepatic cells while the sweet Annie would nourish the liver yin, decreasing the heat and inflammation that caused Jasper to pant and drink, especially at night. The third formula, a traditional Chinese herbal combination, focused on detoxification and the prevention of tumor growth.

Nutraceuticals also played a role in aiding the body's innate healing capacity. I prescribed antioxidants such as selenium, vitamin E, vitamin A/D in the form of cod liver oil, green tea extract and a diet including raw ground parsley, broccoli, burdock root and turkey. I recommended that Jasper not eat wheat, barley, oats, rice or any other grain. Even his treats needed to be grain-free, made of either meat or vegetable.

Wendy asked, "Should we have him on shark cartilage? I've heard that can prevent cancer."

The shark cartilage issue had always been a sore point with me. I pulled out my soapbox. "Many people give their pets shark cartilage to prevent tumors because they believe that sharks are immune to cancer. But actually, sharks are afflicted with tumors," I said, thinking about the research I had read from MIT, revealing that although sharks may secrete an angiogenin inhibitor, there is no evidence that ingesting their cartilage can help treat or prevent cancer. I cringed at the numbers: seventy million sharks were killed annually, an unsustainable harvest to say the least. "How we create our medicine is just as important as the medicine itself," I continued. "I believe that if we formulate our medicine from sustainable sources, harvested with respect and kindness, then our patients will be capable of miraculous healing."

After handing Wendy the three herbal bottles, my handwritten diet and a supplement regime, I sat on the floor next to my patient, gently inserting acupuncture needles into specific points. I focused on my own intent, crowding out any negative thoughts, pouring all of my positive energy into Jasper's treatment. I chose three points on each side of Jasper's body. The first was Triple Heater 2, *Fluid's Door*, a point towards the outside of each front paw that I chose for its role in the generation and distribution of fluids. The second point, Stomach 40, *Abundant Flourishing*, a point located on the outside of each stifle, would soften and drain the phlegm. The third point, Liver 8, *Curved Spring*, located on the inside of each back leg, would regulate the liver and drain its heat.

After ten minutes, I removed all Jasper's needles and the Millers thanked me, optimistically setting up our next session. I finished the appointment by giving Jasper vitamin injections, and then looked at my patient, with his long grey muzzle and a tail that still wagged half-heartedly. I patted rich waves of his thick fur and looked into his eyes for a hint of what tomorrow might bring. Like a guide, I could only suggest a path for his healing, but he would ultimately decide his own fate.

Jasper's spirit seemed to be hovering. "Good and lost," Iris called it, that confusing place between life and death, caught in the decision between healing this sick body or moving on to whatever the next life brings. As a healer of the spirit, my job was to accept any outcome. As Jasper turned to leave, I knelt by his side, holding him the way you might hug a good friend, tight enough to last forever.

A Sense of Direction

EVEN ON THE CLEAREST summer day, I can follow a hiking trail and somehow find myself circling back to where I started, all the while convinced that I am going in the right direction. I do it in shopping malls, too, which is one of the many reasons I avoid them. I can enter a store from one direction, only to backtrack in the same direction, later thinking, *Huh, these stores look kind of familiar*. Particularly adept at denial, I always begin my mountain hikes believing I will not get lost, forgetting about that last time I had to call for help. It's an embarrassing skill and I've been perfecting it for forty-three years. Enter an ocean kayak or a horse into the confusion, along with poor weather conditions, and now you have my life outside my clinic, which is not a lot different from my life in the clinic: a repetitive fluctuation between difficulty and relief.

One summer afternoon, as fog filtered into our rich, sweet forest of red cedar, I decided to ride my ex-racehorse, Charlie, up Sumas Mountain behind our yurt. If the mountain was located back east, people would consider it formidable, but around here, it amounted to little more than a foothill with a complicated crisscrossing of old logging roads. Had Jeff been on the scene with his trusty compass and uncanny pigeon-like knack for finding home, things would have been safer. But as it was, only Smudge accompanied us; I'd given in to her shrill protests at being left behind.

Charlie is petrified of all small things from the natural world, most notably sticks, small birds, large birds like grouse, and even dragonflies. Ironically, things that should scare him don't. Bears don't really faze him, nor do double-wide semi-trucks, but weather patterns drive him berserk—snow, rain, wind and even sun, which brings out all the insects. Each time something catches him off-guard, like a daisy poking up through the grass, all four feet splay out like a saw horse and he springs up, lurching about unpredictably, looking like a cartoon character, eyes wide and hooves in all four directions. And of course there's me, up there hanging on for dear life. Friends have suggested I get a more trail-ready mount, one that doesn't break out in hives the minute May rolls around, but I ride Charlie for the entertainment value and to keep life fresh. Although it may not be the safest hobby, riding a horse alone in nature is one of my most rejuvenating pastimes. Wildlife is less afraid of a human on a horse. Charlie and I once stood face to face with a magnificent buck with antlers like branches, so close I could see our reflection in his eyes.

We headed out, my little dog, Smudge, following Charlie and me, coursing our way through ravines, river valleys and coniferous forests of second-growth fir and cedar. Named by the Native Americans "tree of life," the bark of the cedar appeared particularly deep orange-red that day. Depending upon my mood, its boughs sometimes resembled a Victorian skirt. But on that day, the cedar was reminiscent of a row of soft green feathers, each one drooping atop another, forming layers of green plumage in delicate curtains. The Douglas fir trees had stubby sharp needles that projected from branches like fingers, each pointing in a slightly different direction. If nature ruled over the greed of logging companies, I thought, these cedars and firs would grow to monstrous sizes.

My thoughts centered around botanical questions. *Is that a wood or lady fern? Can I tell a cottonwood from a maple by its bark? Is that a large salmonberry or an elderberry?* The world of plants held many mysteries. Preoccupied with investigating native plants along the path, I scarcely noticed the increasing fog, slowly becoming so dense that, after two hours, we had doubled back in the wrong direction.

It was starting to get dark so I dropped Charlie's reins to the buckle, relaxed my legs and left him free to go wherever he wanted. I hoped to create a moment of understanding in my trusty steed, so that he could depend on whatever vestige of instinctive sense of direction might remain, his pre-racing thinking cap. I hoped that eventually he might lead us home. But Charlie just stood there, staring straight ahead, all four hooves planted uncharacteristically on the ground. Charlie's giant ribcage expanded beneath me and he chewed on his bit, settling into waiting mode. He was a horse with virtually no survival skills and way too much faith in me. I finally gave up, took up the reins and proceeded to get us more lost.

After reviewing my dwindling options, I started to look for a place to settle down for the night. At that moment, Smudge ran out in front of Charlie as if to say "I know the way back!" So we followed her little black head around corners, across streams and apparently down the mountain. Smudge would occasionally peer back at us, her overgrown ears perched expectantly like wings, bouncing with her new-found responsibility. At the edge of ravines, deep river beds and gullies, Smudge waited for us, bolting forward when we caught up.

Because I am an expert at getting lost, I can say from experience that the moment you feel the most lost is often followed by a moment of clarity. After an hour, just when I was about to doubt Smudge's navigation abilities, I saw the outline of our round house in a backdrop of misty clouds. I looked up at the green canopy of trees and the last bit of light, thankful for Smudge's sense of direction. I longed to hold on to her strong-willed essence, that opinionated edge I usually cursed. As we rode into the barn, she trotted in, leading the way. Proud. Confident. Terrier. She had led us home.

Five years ago, before we had started dating, Jeff and I took a kayak trip through the San Juan Islands. As we quietly paddled through the emerald green water, a soft breeze swept over the boats and a grey-spotted seal followed the bubbles in our wake. For seven years, Jeff and I had been kayaking buddies, secure enough in our friendship to give advice to one another. And I surely needed it. "Are you sure you know where we're going?" Jeff asked, seeing that I had led us to an island rather than a peninsula. To say Jeff was understated would be an understatement. So he probably knew we were lost but would patiently follow me into open ocean if necessary.

I wondered if everyone in Minnesota had a built-in compass like Jeff did, and if his navigational intuition had anything to do with the flat terrain, long stretches of snow and ice or the lack of memorable landmarks in his home state. On his canoe trips in northern Minnesota, one island looked just like another and you needed a special kind of instinct to distinguish between them.

Jeff's wilderness survival and directional skills came from his father, a man who'd think nothing of squashing a half-dozen ticks with his fork at the dinner table before eating his salad. During summer vacations, father and son would charter a floatplane and travel up to isolated rivers in northern Quebec where you're more likely to see caribou than another person. On the rare occasion when there weren't larger fish to catch, they would trap sticklebacks (the wilderness equivalent of sardines) with their bare hands and pick wild blueberries for dessert. Some days, they were "winded out," stuck in their tent, unable to paddle against gusty storms. They were also forced to stay in their tent at dusk to avoid nighttime raids of mosquitoes and black flies. The small insects would crawl into their socks with bites so itchy that sleep was futile. To this day, on camping trips, Jeff still tucks squares of paper towels into his right rear pocket, his dad's answer to toilet paper which falls apart the minute it gets wet. Comfort to a Minnesotan might be interpreted as misery to most anyone else.

Jeff and I met through a mutual patient, a self-mutilating malamute that had developed multiple hot spots and deep fissures from hours of compulsive licking. Jeff recommended acupuncture after months of unsuccessful conventional treatments. Having long been interested in Asian philosophy, Jeff had a natural affinity for traditional Chinese medicine. After three acupuncture treatments gave the large dog significant relief, Jeff came to my office to watch my procedure of *surrounding the dragon*, in which I encircled the dog's red lesion with acupuncture needles. At lunch, we talked about his childhood journeys into the Canadian wilderness. I was fascinated by his stories of navigating swift rivers, portaging around waterfalls and paddling along primitive shorelines.

As our kayak paddles dipped into the salty kelp-filled water of Puget Sound, I realized that we both happened to be single at the same time. I looked over at Jeff to see his patient face in the shadow of his wide-brimmed kayak hat, a brown curled ponytail hanging over the back of his lifejacket. Although he still arose early each morning for his daily meditation, Jeff no longer held to a strict schedule of bed at eight and morning meditation at five. With his increasingly relaxed lifestyle, I thought there might be room for my animals and me in his life. I cleared my throat and opened my mouth, the way you do when you're about to put your foot in it. "So, have you ever thought of us getting together?" I heard the question but couldn't believe I was the one asking it.

"No, not really," he answered, paddling off in front, his boat dipping into a large rolling wave. But then he smiled and I knew that was Minnesotan for, "Yes, I've been thinking of being with you for years." With an eagle soaring overhead, we sat close together on a pebbled beach. As he turned to kiss me, I felt relieved that after seven years of friendship, it didn't feel as though I were kissing my brother. From the beach we looked out at our boats and the slowly rising tide that lifted them into its wake. With the swirl of our new emotions, our boats tilted towards one another in the gentle surf. Even though we now entered the murky waters of a relationship, nothing felt more natural.

Where I had been messy and disorganized, Jeff was neat and orderly; when I confused one island for another, he unfolded and straightened his waterproof map of Puget Sound, wiping off bits of seaweed, to set me straight. Within a year, Jeff and I were married and his clean and crumb and relatively hair-free world was about to change.

Follow Your Nose

TO MY SURPRISE and relief, Jasper survived the week. Now, according to Wendy, he was having a few good days, time seemingly stolen back from his cancer, giving us a remote hope that we had suspended a downward spiral. I saw him for his second appointment on a sunny Monday afternoon. As he entered my office, rather than dragging his back toes, he walked in fairly normally, lifted his head occasionally and proceeded to sniff all four corners of the room. Rather than the deep brick red of the week before, his tongue color was now a lavender pink, suggesting that his overall circulation and body temperature had improved.

Even with these signs of improvement, though, Jasper was still extremely underweight and very weak. His eyes remained dull, and the nominal amount of weight he had gained was a result of accumulating abdominal fluid produced by his leaking tumors. Attempting to remove the fluid presented multiple problems and would only give him short-term relief. Again, we were left with few possible medical treatments, reminding me of climbing a steep slope above the tree line, grabbing small twigs only to rip them out of the ground; so few medical options, so few big trees left to hold on to.

"I hope he improves a little more this week," Wendy said, her eyes puffy and tired. "We enrolled him in a nose work class when we learned he had cancer."

She read my puzzled look. "After the diagnosis, we enrolled Jasper in a training program for nose work. We hoped it might help him stay mentally and physically stimulated." The idea was to encourage and develop a dog's natural scenting abilities and innate desire to hunt a target odor. In the process, the dogs have fun, building confidence and focus while burning mental and physical energy. It was not normally the place you'd find a dog with such a serious health condition.

But Jasper had spent his life as a natural seeker. The Millers often took Jasper with them on kayak trips. When they paddled to shore, the dog would bound from his bucket seat onto the beach. Immediately, he'd begin to dig, pawing so aggressively at the sand that it flew out behind him. After an hour, he would proudly lay in the middle of a twenty-foot-long trench, happily gnawing on a stick to celebrate his masterpiece of excavation.

All of my medical training told me that Jasper should be inside a bubble, isolated from infectious disease and confined to the house to prevent the rupture of his tumors. Sick dogs, I had learned, should be quietly resting at home. But then, rules were meant to be broken. I remember reading Temple Grandin's book, *Animals Make Us Human*. She highlighted the importance of *seeking*: looking forward to an activity or object. When an animal's attention is in a playful, seeking mode, he or she cannot simultaneously feel fear. Seeking is a necessary emotion that is often devoid in many animals' lives, especially after a grave diagnosis. Jasper's nose work class would provide him with a new form of seeking, and instead of obsessing over his tumors, the Millers could let his new focus alleviate their own fear as well. I imagined Jasper barking and wagging his tail when he picked up the scent of birch oil in a little metal box hidden in the back yard. Jasper's seeking behavior would be just as important to his overall health as any herbal therapy.

When I was young, I unknowingly implemented this idea of seeking with my own dog, Julietta. Just after we adopted her from a litter of sick puppies at the shelter, she broke with bloody diarrhea. As we waited for the veterinarian, I held her in my lap, upside down in a blue blanket as though she were a doll. I looked around the waiting room and noticed other people staring off into space: a slumping old man, a young woman in plaid jeans and a wool scarf, a couple holding a baby carrier on one side and a beagle on the other. Their pets were quietly protesting from within carriers or crouching fearfully under chairs. Julietta and I looked at one another. She was weak and her eyes gazed up at me for a clue to her destiny. Three black eyebrow whiskers followed my every move. Owing to my mother's amazing ability to work despite almost any disturbance, she sat next to us reading and correcting students' final exams, making big swirls with her red pen.

Thinking back to that veterinary clinic, I can still remember the exam room, the perky technicians and the doctor's white lab coat and grim face as he reported Julietta's poor prognosis. Parvovirus had struck her small, malformed, basset-like body, and her only beautiful feature, the darkened liner around her brown eyes, now drooped as she hung her head on the steel exam table. "The smell," the veterinarian said, "is unmistakable." His eyes shifted to the clock when a cat howled in a back room.

My mother was speechless at the diagnosis, not because she loved the puppy even an eighth as much as I did, but because we were facing the death of an immediate family member for the first time, and were completely unprepared for it. The veterinarian suggested putting Julietta to sleep, no doubt because he correctly assumed that we could not afford hospitalization, and even if we could, her future looked bleak.

Looking back, it seems to me that his recommendation for euthanasia was premature and that he just wanted to worry about one less puppy and get on with his day. I imagine his world was so full of suffering that it was easier to let Julietta go than try to save her. Perhaps to him, death meant peace. But at that age, I didn't know what it meant. In the 1970s, euthanasia may have seemed painless compared to what we all saw on television, back when news seemed less biased, when we were haunted by visions of war. Eventually, years later, it would be me on the doctor side of the exam table, afraid of failing, afraid of letting people down, afraid of encouraging false hope.

It was then that my twelve-week-old puppy looked up at me pleadingly, giving a last tiny wag of her tail. My mother looked up from her pile of ungraded exams and silently nodded her tacit semi-approval. Even she noticed the puppy's hint of hope. Right or wrong, this decision would be left to me, even though I may have been too young to make it. "Doctor," I said with a small voice and a lump in my throat, "I'd like to try to save her at home." Confusion filled the exam room with its smell of rubbing alcohol and sick puppy.

The veterinarian looked at my mother's face for a more sensible decision, but when none came, he said, "Okay, young lady, you've got to work hard at this, and even then, she might not make it."

Although thirty years later, Julietta's veterinarian might have been sued for giving so many pills to a nine-year-old, back then, he thought nothing of handing me the plastic prescription bottles and showing me how to pinch the puppy's skin to check for dehydration. With no fanfare, I tucked Julietta back under her towel, and carried her out to our dented blue car while my mother paid the bill. I didn't know it then, but she had cashed in some family heirlooms and old coins to pay for this unforeseen expense.

Before and after school, I treated the small puppy. Sometimes I felt the hopelessness in it, while other times my determination took over. Every day I'd race home to find her waiting for me. I'd clean up the bloody diarrhea on the newspaper-lined kitchen floor that we walled off especially for her. Then I'd give her canned food and water through a large syringe as her pale tongue lapped it up. Afterward, I'd gently pry open her mouth to slide a huge blue pill as far down her throat as possible. After a few days of no improvement and minimal appetite, she hung her head as though the force of gravity weighed heavier on her than on anyone else. I asked my mother to let Julietta sleep with me, imagining that if I could hold her cold body close to me, I'd be able to warm her up. Naturally, with the putrid nature of Julietta's stools, Mom resisted my request for a while, but I explained that there was a medical point to it.

Even with her medications and round-the-clock nursing care, Julietta was still unwilling to eat on her own. I decided to try a new technique to stimulate her appetite, hiding small pieces of chicken in various places throughout my room. At first, she appeared uninterested, but gradually her nose began twitching with the allure of appetizing scents lurking from under the covers, behind the bed and in an old pair of dress shoes. Each day, I added larger pieces to our new seeking game. And over the next few days, Julietta's appetite slowly returned. Within a month, she had rounded a corner, gradually returning to her normal playful self.

I thought of Julietta's remarkable recovery from parvovirus as I sat contemplating Jasper's precarious health. "Wendy, maybe you're on to something with this nose work," I said. "But, if possible, try to keep Jasper from jumping around too much." Among other concerns, I worried that any heavy exertion could cause the tumors to bleed. Wendy promised that all his initial training would be done on flat terrain. I continued, "Just in case, let's add another Chinese patent herb, Yunnan pao yao, to his herbal regime. It aids in blood clotting and might help keep his tumors from bleeding."

As I inserted acupuncture needles into important liver-strengthening points, Wendy shared her trick of combining all Jasper's powdered herbs and vitamins in a turkey baster and then briskly rubbing him down with a towel to get him excited about taking the gruel. "If I use the towel to fluff up and down his back, he gets so excited and happy, he barely realizes he's taking any medicine at all!"

With the needles in place, I sat back and watched him relax

into his acupuncture treatment. I asked myself what else I could do to strengthen his immune system. The answer to my question was an herb first introduced to me one summer in the Cascade Mountains by my herbal teacher, Madsu, a thin, grey-haired man reminiscent of an elf. With a wildcrafter's permit—a guarantee that no plant would be over-harvested—Madsu had silently walked through the forest carrying a heavy burlap sack slung over his left shoulder. As I followed him, I had to look up occasionally to be sure I had not veered off his path, sucked accidentally into a patch of salal.

We climbed over huge logs covered with green sheets of elk moss and usnea lichen. Dirt built up and caked onto our knees as we knelt in front of some rattlesnake plantain, investigating its vibrant white center vein. The air was damp and cold. Droplets fell when I exhaled and each breath made me feel more alive.

Madsu stopped abruptly to admire and bless his favorite plant, ocean spray, a large bush also known as ironwood because bows and arrows were made from its sturdy pith. I watched him place sacred red willow bark beside its base. To him, the bush represented the survival of his people, and indeed, it was a shrub worthy of notice. With a collection of small, energetic white flowers extending proudly into the sky, it resembled the spray of the sea crashing against a rocky shoreline. Each of its leaves was decorated with fine ridges in circular fan-like patterns, the leaf margin as wavy as water, reminding me of the thrill of a storm at sea.

Pieces of cedar crumbled into our hair as we ducked under a large rotten stump to find turkey tail mushrooms, a shelved cluster of woody fantails, brown and orange-tinted with a white underbelly. When one hikes with a mushroom expert and herbalist, every rotten log becomes a subject worthy of special treatment, full of hidden clues. Unlike plants, mushrooms are only present for a few days, sometimes only a few hours, so you have to leave your worries, your lists and your disagreements with others all behind and focus on that bounty of mushrooms. Known as an immune modulator, turkey tail is one of many medicinal mushrooms that help the immune system recognize and kill cancer cells.

Madsu sought wild herbs by day and made medicine by night. We spent hours gathering reishi and turkey tail, chiseling at the mushrooms and then slinging the wood-like fungus into our burlap sacks. Our other sacks contained sheets of fluffy, light green usnea rolled on long sticks like cotton candy, and chunks of precious red root, an herb whose potency increases as its environment becomes more hostile. When we returned to our camp on a hillside outside Twisp, the moon gave us just enough light to layer some of our herbs onto thin racks and place them into a large dryer. Then we began crushing the mushrooms, tincturing them immediately, and pouring the liquid into large amber bottles to retain their medicinal potency.

Madsu learned how to gather medicine and process it from his mother, who traced her native roots to a Spokane woman named Teshwintichina. From her, he also learned how to make cakes from camas, bitterroot and black tree lichen. Camas bulb needed to be baked long enough to release the sweet inulin; an hour too early and it would still be bitter; an hour too late and it would turn to mush. The black lichen was packed into cakes when it was still a warm sticky substance that could be molded easily. His family would cook the camas on warm summer nights when song and fire could pass the hours. They could smell when their camas had cooked long enough to convert the inulin. They could smell when medicine was ready.

To me, many of Madsu's herbal and food preparation practices seemed witch-like, entrenched in fire-born ritual. But I later discovered that some of the plants' active ingredients, so important for immune-modulation, disappeared quickly without quick preparation. They were also more bioactive in the beginning of the autumn when the leaves of the alder tree start to turn gold. The ability to know when to harvest one plant based on the life cycle of another made sense when one lived in community with the plants, truly understanding their annual rhythms.

Jasper understood annual rhythms too. In the summer, he hunted for moles in the fields. As fall approached, he sniffed out and ate blackberries. As Christmas approached, he dutifully protected the house, bravely fending off evil delivery truck drivers.

And unlike the unsophisticated Yorkie next door, he didn't fall for their clever dog biscuit tricks.

Back at the clinic, I left Wendy and Jasper in the exam room while I reached up in my herbal pharmacy for a bottle of turkey tail and reishi made by Madsu that September night. I thought of how the field we'd chosen to make medicines smelled of sweet tarragon after a moist evening, and how Madsu blessed the medicine, completely present with his full attention on healing. The stars had beamed over our makeshift laboratory on a deeply nourishing night and the nearly full moon floated overhead as we worked on counters of cut logs, swirling jars of herbal menstruum.

"Let's start him on this mushroom blend," I suggested, handing Wendy an amber bottle, just as herbalists have done for generations. As they all got up to leave at the end of the appointment, I saw the tip of Jasper's dry, cracked nose sniff at a liver treat I had cradled in my palm. At that point, I could see a trace of his inner life force, not through a brightness in his eyes, but through a twitch of his nose.

Superstition

DURING MY FOUR YEARS of veterinary school, I returned home to western Washington only occasionally. So I was surprised when one fall day in my junior year, I received a call from Iris. She told me that I was the only one she trusted to move her beloved comfrey, a forty-year-old plant with an integrated collection of round roots, some the size of Clydesdale's hooves. Apparently her nephew who lived in a nearby town needed a longer driveway and a new garage to house his new sports car. So even though she believed that moving the established plant brought bad luck, we nonetheless began shoveling soil together on a mild autumn weekend.

"I remember moving my mother's comfrey," she said, quietly. Although she still sounded like the old Iris, I knew by her lackluster brown sweater and slacks that something was just not right. "I was only five when Mom was forced to dig it up, only to die a year later," she sighed, shoveling half-heartedly. "My uncle said it was her heart. She looked so healthy before she moved that plant, but then she got weaker by the day."

I didn't buy all that superstition. It had no basis in science. And I was currently enthralled with modern diagnostic tools and all that we doctors could offer. After all, I had been surrounded by it for the last three years. In veterinary school, I helped care for an Arabian mare with a fracture of the left front limb. Most horses with fractures above the knee are euthanized immediately because no repair can bear their weight. But with the tools of modern medicine, cast changes and repeated radiographs, along with this particular mare's special kind of patience with months of immobilization, she was healing.

Ours was a family of scientists, naturally prone to ask obscure questions, albeit on vastly different subjects. Holidays provided a break from our everyday lives: my brother's busy laboratory, my mother's international studies, and my fascination with physiology. My brother had become a full-fledged chemistry professor, analyzing cancer proteins with a mass spectrometer, so our holiday conversations often veered from peace talks in Macedonia to top-down proteomics, an in-depth form of protein analysis my brother had invented. At Thanksgiving, Neil would expound on the complexities of distinctive carbon bonds. Bewilderment wracked my mother and grandmother, as they had no formal training in chemistry. And even with two and a half years of college chemistry under my belt, I could still barely follow him. He would say something about an electrospray, magnetic force and the unique weight of the molecules along a circular path, but I couldn't make out the details nor figure out how it related to the future of cancer treatment. Fortunately, my patients in vet school offered some good middle-ground conversation.

My grandmother chimed in, her face eagerly anticipating a good story over mashed potatoes. "So, Donna, what animals have you saved recently?" I'd tell them about healing the mare's broken leg or suturing a Maltese's deep laceration. When Gramma got sick of hearing about the pros and cons of each suture style, her head bobbing as she fought off sleep, I piqued her interest again with stories about the intensive care unit. I explained how I once helped resuscitate a German shepherd after his heart had stopped. A group of interns had descended upon his stretcher after a nasty car accident. One veterinarian performed chest compressions, while another quickly inserted an intravenous catheter. But I, I was the one who connected the electrocardiogram, shaving four neat square patches on each of his legs. I swabbed alcohol where it connected to the skin with one hand, while injecting medications to counter the dog's cardiovascular shock with the other. After only a few days in the hospital, the dog went home with his elated owner who promised to buy a leash.

Iris had little interest in my stories or my blossoming knowledge of science. When I tried to tell her about the mare or the shepherd, she turned away, more interested in digging up a mallow weed than in an abnormal ECG. In Iris's garden, just the idea of moving a plant with such a strong affinity to the earth felt wrong, and I cringed when we dug up the comfrey's large, succulent roots. It was nothing like moving a mint, a plant capable of growing tiny roots from almost anywhere on its stem, with only a trace of water needed to facilitate sprouting. It's not that the comfrey didn't move on its own accord; it spread readily underground by rhizomes. But when it settled somewhere, it wanted to stay and bind itself to the earth through its gourd-like root tubers.

It was a mournful event to be sure. All the other medicinal plants had faded now that Iris had lost her youthful spark. I stopped to brush off an earthworm from the sticky brown clay. Even if we damaged the root, the comfrey plant would most likely survive. But we wanted to preserve its grandeur and give respect to it as though it were a family elder. So we brushed at the borders of its round roots as delicately as archaeologists unveiling a Neanderthal skull.

Despite Iris's somber nature, it was nice to be digging in the dirt again. I felt the sun on my face and marveled at the sturdiness of Iris's meadow rue, a plant thought to accompany the spirit when the body dies. Even I had to admit that its leaves looked whimsical. Rue seemed to laugh at big problems, laugh at my midterm surgery exam, laugh at my student loans. Rue relished its carefree nature, its lacy leaves giggling in the wind.

As I looked at the large comfrey leaves, some over two feet long and a foot wide, I decided it was a plant that took life seriously and wanted to be noticed, often delivering a nasty rash with its sturdy sandpaper leaves. Honeybees covered every pink and purple flower, and in the summer, the plant buzzed all day. Even though plenty of Europeans brought comfrey to North America, owing to its propensity to heal wounds and bones, Iris still spoke of her plant as though it were a shriveled raisin of a thing we'd never be able to resuscitate.

"I recall the folks cured by this very plant," she said, as a few splotches of dirt made their way to her jaw and down her wrinkled neck, just like the old days when I was still a teenager, both of us oblivious to the flecks of soil covering our faces and clothes.

I saw my old friend living in the past, and it concerned me. "Iris, has anyone stopped by lately?" I asked, thinking about Helen or even the neighbors.

"People are too busy these days. We live in a plantless world," she replied in a drone that even bored the cats.

"Maybe you can start a new social movement," I suggested optimistically. Even though it was not yet my dream, it hurt me to see that she could not live hers: to share plants with the neighbors, borrowing garden tools and having someone who wanted her extra zucchini instead of letting it rot. The suburbs had squashed the dream out of her. Now only the plants provided her with company. They were dependable year after year.

I looked up from my shovel to see her gazing past me, past the rows of brown and drooped plant skeletons that surrounded us. "If people realized money isn't everything, if they cared about plants and nature, then I'd see eye to eye with them. We need the old communities, but they are gone," she said, drifting off again.

"Remember all the people you cured with your herbs?" I asked, hoping to focus on the positive role she had played in our lives.

"Yeah," she said, after a few minutes of thought. "There was old Jack down the street with that big cut on his arm, remember that guy? He was such a big guy but couldn't handle an ounce of pain." She brightened with the memory of healing. I never met Jack but I knew the tincture, poultice and salve that she used to treat his wound. She kept it on the upper left shelf of her pantry just in case anyone got hurt.

If Iris's salves proved effective, it was because she was so meticulous in their preparation, a fact I'd curse many a summer afternoon when I'd rather be caring for my animals. She'd quiz me as we bent over the orange and yellow calendula flowers. "Okay, feel this flower. Is it ready?" she would ask, clutching the clippers in her palm. She taught me to feel for the resins in its sticky petals. "Remember, always harvest calendula in the afternoon when most of the resins have gathered to the bottom of the flower." When I confirmed that it was ready, we clipped forty flowers and wilted them in the sun, evaporating the excess moisture.

"What about this Hypericum?" she would then ask, referring to the St. John's wort, a plant with bright yellow flowers. Using a magnifying loop she had given me one Christmas, I examined each petal carefully. Tiny perforated holes covered each yellow petal, giving *Hypericum perforatum* a name that made sense. A small purple sac accompanied each hole. Iris said that when the sac darkened and became richer in color, the plant was ready to harvest. We collected it with the last of the salmon berries. Iris beamed. "Better to pick Hypericum in the evening when the dew releases its healing," she said. After a few weeks, all the herbs had been harvested and packed in clear glass jars filled with olive oil. She placed them in a south-facing sand box to ensure they'd reach ninety degrees, insisting on infusing the oils with the sun's warmth instead of hastening the process on the stove.

Then in August, after weeks of occasionally mixing the oils

and setting them back into the sand, each jar achieved its desired rich color. The calendula oil turned a deep orange-yellow while the comfrey took on the rich green color of moss. Then there were the bright colors I could never predict. Although both plants had yellow flowers, infused St. John's wort oil turned bright tomato-soup red, while the essential oil of chamomile turned a beautiful sky blue.

But the most important thing to Iris was the beeswax necessary to solidify and preserve the salves. She insisted that it come from Helen Benstead because she was one of the few beekeepers who did not use chemicals. Every August, I biked to Helen's house and tucked the fragrant, creamy yellow bricks of beeswax into my pocket as if they were gold. When we finished pouring the heated wax into the oil, Iris lined her porch with a hundred or so one-ounce amber jars. After checking each salve's consistency to see if it clung to the knife when cooled, with a steady and experienced hand, she poured her salves. It was the only time she locked the cats in her back bedroom, preventing the playful and mischievous cats from batting her jars around for attention, leaving imprints of their whiskers and noses on the surface of her otherwise perfect finished product. At the end, we'd celebrate by eating fresh watermelon, the delicious juice dripping down our chins and onto our shirts. Her spirit was so vibrant back then. She wouldn't even think of moving a single plant for a sports car, much less her beloved comfrey.

But there we were, placing the comfrey in large buckets, moving its roots, stem, leaves and flowers in heavy sections. Although she advised drinking small amounts of comfrey tea for healing fractures and deep injuries, the FDA had recently banned it for internal use, claiming its pyrrolizidine alkaloids caused liver disease in some people. She shook her head. "Once the plant flowers, it contains almost none of those toxins," she said. "If the FDA really cared about people, they would make drinking alcohol and smoking tobacco against the law." Later, I looked up the statistics: alcohol killed 50,000 annually, and tobacco killed 450,000. When she was younger, Iris thought the whole world was against her but she didn't care. Now she seemed so vulnerable, as though her nettles had lost their sting. We dug in silence for awhile and I wondered why I wasn't back in Pullman studying for Monday's surgery lab.

"Why do we have to dig up the comfrey? Why can't he store the car somewhere else?" I asked, but Iris gazed off blankly at the clouds, her face grey and dull in the shade of her old cedar tree.

"My nephew is taking the house when I go. All my affairs are put to rest now. I did what I could in this life," she said, leaving me speechless. Veterinary school gave me little training in how to prepare for the end of life. But I could see that Iris had finished her work. All the herbal tinctures stored in the pantry for winter, the mullein already harvested and the comfrey and Oregon grape root tea cooled and ready to apply. Now she turned matters over to the plants. But none of it seemed right to me.

As we collected the large round roots, Iris's old cat, Tinkerbelle, walked by. She looked weak and frail, much too thin for a simple diagnosis of old age. "Iris, do you mind if I take her to Doc Simpson for a blood test?" I asked, secretly hoping for the refusal I'd come to expect regarding conventional medicine and Dr. Simpson in particular. But she gave me no argument.

So I loaded Tinkerbelle into my car and drove down the road to the small veterinary clinic. Dr. Simpson examined Tinkerbelle and drew a blood sample. In just short of an hour, he gave me the results. Her kidneys were failing. He told me her long-term prognosis was not good. Based on her severe dehydration, weight loss and abnormal lab values, he felt that she had been sick for quite a long time.

Later, I confronted Iris. "Why didn't you take her to the vet earlier?" She acknowledged my question and apologized but I could tell her heart was not in it. I could see she was letting go of all she once loved and it frustrated me. After all, the cat needed fluids, vitamins, a special diet and plenty of access to water. She was getting none of those things here. I agreed to take Tinkerbelle back to school with me, and, once she improved, to return her to Iris.

In the months that followed, I turned my sparse veterinary school apartment into a makeshift hospital: bags of fluids hanging from poles, unused needles lining the counters, a half-dozen empty cans of prescription food beside the sink, and a cat in the windowsill staring blankly outside, longing for missed afternoons in the comfrey.

One Veterinarian's Opinion

OUR GREEN YURT is tucked back in the conifers and Jeff and I often enjoy the gentle summer sway of cedar boughs off our back deck. Living in a round space is inspiring. There is a circular flow of energy through our home, and when we look out the tall picture windows at Stewart Mountain, we are reminded that we are part of nature.

One summer day, shortly after we had moved into our home, Jeff and I talked about our similar medical philosophies and the relative importance of Eastern and Western medicine. For fractures, intestinal blockages, dehydration or bloat, conventional veterinarians served a vital role in saving animals. But there were others: patients with minor gastrointestinal symptoms, hot spots or intermittent lamenesses—animals that were capable of healing on their own with a subtle nudge in the right direction. Both Jeff and I had faith in the body's fundamental ability to heal itself, believing that not every successful outcome was the result of a doctor's intervention.

"Someone brought in a vomiting beagle today," Jeff said, warming up the grill to prepare for our guests that evening.

"Did you have to run blood work or radiographs?" I asked, adding fistfuls of ice to a large cooler on the deck. We both knew the possible rule-outs—foreign body obstructions, poisoning, pancreatitis, liver or kidney problems.

"No, the exam was pretty normal. He probably just got into the garbage. I told them to keep him off food for the day and then feed him a bland diet for the next few days." That meant he'd place a follow-up call tomorrow to be sure the beagle had improved. Many times, with no treatment at all, his patient made a full recovery.

We had invited a group of veterinarians, including a former classmate named Dorrie, to our yurt for grilled oyster mushrooms, veggie kebabs and lentil burgers. It happened to be the day after a Rottweiler bit Dorrie's hand, which was now wrapped in thick gauze. Everyone practiced conventional medicine except me, and

110

all but Jeff were women. Although the food was good, our guests probably would have come just for the frothy beer, cold and numbing on a warm summer night.

In an effort to establish some camaraderie amidst our differences in medical philosophies, Jeff said in a chipper voice, "Donna was also bit by a dog. It was an Afghan, right, honey?" Everyone looked to me to fill in the details of the ordeal. Instinctively, I held my palm up to the right side of my cheek, where the scar still lingered, a nasty half-moon crease that fortunately blended into the smile lines around my mouth. I explained that this particular dog was a show dog that wore booties on his paws and a bonnet around his head, most of his day spent either in a crate or being meticulously combed and groomed. In other words, this Afghan harbored a lot of pent-up anxieties.

That dog, and the millions of show dogs like him, hinted at the reason Jeff and I didn't think the movie *Best in Show* was funny. We had watched it a few years before, stone-faced, as our non-vet friends roared with laughter, doubling over in the aisles. "Do you like this movie?" he whispered, and when I shrugged, we left the theater early. Neither of us slept well that night. It was troubling to see show dogs with no lives or decisions of their own, spending much of their day crated up in the back of an SUV.

Recalling the day of my bite wound, I said, "It happened so

fast. When I saw blood dripping on my hand, I panicked, thinking it was the dog's blood." But twenty-five sutures later, it looked like I had been in a nasty bar fight. I had to drink my liquefied dinner of chickpeas and green beans through a straw.

One of the other veterinarians piped up, her face wrinkled from years of working as a veterinarian. "I hate it when the dogs don't warn you. If they bit anyone else, the owner might be sued, and the dog euthanized. But if a dog or cat bites us, it often doesn't get reported. It's just part of the job."

As the conversation turned into a gripe session, I disappeared from the group, carrying Smudge outside through a side door, something I did multiple times a day without thought. At eighteen years old, the grey-faced black terrier's strong attitude had outlasted her bladder. I took off her diaper, accustomed to watching as she wandered in circles. Dementia had taken hold of her and she could now only see shadows, but I knew she still recognized Jeff and me, probably by our scents. Her appetite continued to thrive into old age and she still lifted her right leg to urinate, a vestige of her youth.

Ironically, one of the many reasons I did not want a human baby was the thought of diapers. Deciding between cloth or disposable might keep me awake at night, each option fraught with the potential for environmental contamination. "How long are babies in diapers?" I had asked Dorrie, never dreaming Smudge would live so long. I had been changing her diapers four times a day for two years, and usually a few of them hung on the fence to dry in the sun, their elastic and tail holes stretched from overuse. When Dorrie informed me that most babies stop wearing diapers after two years, I felt a bit jealous, since my sleep was still interrupted on many nights by the smell of dog urine.

As I lifted my elderly terrier up onto the patio, underestimating the shockwave we created just by our very presence, I looked at the faces of my veterinary colleagues; the expressions ranged from mildly shocked to appalled. Jeff was the only one who seemed unflustered, still munching on some chips. "Donna, how long are you going to keep Smudge going?" Dorrie asked. The patio fell silent. I thought of my harsh criticism of Iris's lack of care for Tinkerbelle, but now the judgment had been turned on me.

"She still eats her homemade diet and happily chews on watermelon rinds," I insisted, defending my opinion to keep Smudge going. As if I were back in veterinary school fighting for the effectiveness of acupuncture, I passionately fought off the idea of my own dog's euthanasia. I still saw a dog that lived a rich life, whose mind I could read through her eyes and expression. I could no longer share in her world the way I had for eighteen years. But I felt that her life was still worth living. The more connected I became with Smudge's spirit, the less I wanted to interfere with her normal aging process, or with her body and spirit slowly parting ways. Euthanasia would split the two as an ax splits wood.

"Are you keeping her alive just for you?" Dorrie said, clearing her bangs with her wrapped hand as though it were a boxing glove. "I realize how hard it must be since you've had her most of your adult life." Indeed, it had been difficult. There were days I was so exhausted, I considered putting Smudge to sleep. A syringe of euthanasia solution sat in the cupboard ready for duty. If I considered my own happiness and the deep wrinkles I had developed since I stopped sleeping through the night, resigned to two a.m. parades around the driveway, euthanasia began to seem reasonable.

But I spent many hours looking into Smudge's pinched and expressionless face. I moved beyond her crusty ocular discharge and dull, white muzzle and into her eyes, the spirit behind the haze. Had Smudge's deterioration been rapid, it might have affected her more dramatically, but instead she remained as determined as ever to walk, eat and be close to me.

"I don't keep her alive for me," I said, although no one actually believed me. I paused, knowing I should stop there, but in keeping with the terrier inside me, I continued. "Don't you ever think we might recommend euthanasia for our clients' animals just a little too early?" I looked up from Smudge to my reluctant audience. "Well, now that animal is mine."

As the veterinarians quickly changed the subject and began discussing the pros and cons of therapeutic cold lasers, I considered life from Smudge's perspective. Instead of hiking in the mountains as she did through her fifteenth year, she now meandered in circles to the right. Instead of sitting by her food bowl, now she gazed upward or into the corners of the room at mealtime. And instead of nestling under my covers to be close, she waited impatiently to feel the comfort of my hand or a warm towel. But in the end, her spiritual journey was her own.

After everyone had finished their meals and left, I wrapped Smudge up in a towel, just like I had done the first few months after I adopted her. But this time, instead of submissive urine, I cleaned dried food off her face and eyes, and brought her back in the house. "Jeff," I asked, as he was cleaning up the grill, "why are veterinarians so quick to recommend euthanasia?"

While Jeff might have chosen to euthanize Smudge already, he respected my opinion and the close bond that she and I had formed through the years. I thought of the last time I had performed euthanasia—it had been in my first years as a veterinarian—and how my stomach churned the minute I touched the syringe full of thick pink fluid. The sense of nausea never left me that day. It's not that I totally disagreed with the practice, but I wondered if we veterinarians could tone down the opinions and offer more options, giving animals something real, something spiritual, something beautiful at the end of life. A proper transition after a life fully lived.

"We don't like thinking about the elderly, or for that matter, the idea of dying at all. When our pets approach the end, we see our own aging in them. It's a mirror we'd like to cover up," Jeff answered, rinsing out bottles and scrubbing dishes. His words echoed in the sink, the water swirling down the drain.

Eventually, months later, we would have to walk down the road of most pet caretakers—the road we all dread. I would end up releasing Smudge from her ailing old body to join forces with the universal light, her unique spirit brightening all that is good in the world. But on this summer night, I helped her find her bed and settle into the soft pressed foam, a form-fitted circle she called home. I worried about the day when I would have to let her go, but for now, I watched as she quietly paddled her feet, dreaming as though she was an earlier version of herself, forging rivers in Idaho's Bitterroot Mountains, digging up molehills in open fields around Chicago and chasing the shadow of a Washington raven. Rather than fearing the decisions of the future, I chose to follow her path of living in the present moment.

The Most
Difficult Decision

ONE MONDAY MORNING, a few months after I began treating Jasper, I received a phone call from his conventional veterinarian. She had examined him the day before and discovered that his tumors were bleeding again, and this time he was so weak that he couldn't even lift his head. The Millers had decided to take Jasper home to spend some time with him and make a decision about what to do next. In his veterinarian's opinion, any hope for his recovery was futile and any attempt at further treatment would be unfair to the patient and confusing to his caretakers.

Then Wendy called.

"He can't pick up his head and he's not moving. Even though they applied an analgesic patch for pain yesterday, he seems more lethargic than ever. I thought we lost him, but I can still see him breathing on our bed," Wendy said, exhausted after another sleepless night.

"Well, I think this might be it," I said, trying to console Wendy while I considered Jasper's worsening condition. "Dr. Roberts called and reported on Jasper's recent blood work, mentioning his liver values have not improved. I don't want him to suffer." I did not want to admit defeat, but the cards were stacked against us once again. Cancer has a way of doing that.

I thought of my other patients who had succumbed to various types of cancer over the past few months: a large Rottweiler with a malignant tumor behind his eye, a black and white tuxedo cat with systemic lymphoma and a shaggy Irish wolfhound with osteosarcoma whose amputation afforded him only a few good months. We often had trouble getting the necessary herbs into those patients and treating them often enough to be effective. It was also sometimes difficult to accurately choose the ideal herbal combination for each individual patient. And even if everything went well, there were still the animals that just plain gave up on this life in favor of another. But Jasper wasn't like that.

Wendy continued, "Well, he's not suffering right now. He's just sleeping. Maybe the pain patch is helping in that way." I thought of the cardinal signs of pain: withdrawing, hunching, clenching the jaw and gazing off with bloodshot distant eyes. But Jasper's lethargic state made it difficult for us to decipher his symptoms. From Wendy's description on the phone, it did sound as though the tumors may have expanded or perforated the liver vasculature. If the mass had ruptured the vena cava, he would have died instantly. I suspected the problem might be that Jasper's abdomen was slowly filling with blood.

Wendy knew pain firsthand. Many years prior, when she was forty, she suffered from the shooting back pains of ankylosing spondylitis. Since little could be done conventionally, she turned to holistic modalities, including tai chi and massage, and now is pain-free. It took years of perseverance to overcome her own chronic disease, so she had patience when it came to her dog's.

The word "patch" repeated itself in my mind: *patch, patch, patch*. As much as I tried to shake off the unsettling mantra, it came back to me again. I lit up with the dim possibility of an alternative explanation.

"What kind of patch? A Fentanyl patch?" I asked.

"Yes," she said.

I remembered reading an article describing some potentially serious side effects with transdermal Fentanyl patches. "The rate at which dogs receive this drug through the skin is highly variable.

So, it's possible that the patch could be causing his symptoms," I said. "Since his signs sound more like weakness than pain, let's try removing the patch and see what happens." Wendy agreed and said she would call me later that afternoon. After I hung up the phone, I realized that now, having acted, I needed to accept whatever might happen. I knew the next few hours would determine Jasper's fate. I imagined Wendy gently massaging his back, cupping his tufted paw between her palms. The concepts of pain and euthanasia swirled in my mind.

Many years ago, when I first began veterinary practice, my boss, a classic old-timer, truly did not believe animals felt pain the way humans do. Of course, in the early nineties, there were no prescription anti-inflammatories available for dogs, so treatment for pain was largely not offered. Although no one can verify exactly what animals feel, I believe they feel the same physical pain that people do but are fortunately spared from the high level of mental and emotional suffering created by their human counterparts.

Now we have swung full circle, owing to the power of the pharmaceutical industry. We aggressively treat many patients for pain, even when we do so mainly to placate their human guardians. For patients with good organ function, pain medication may be relatively benign. But because of Jasper's compromised liver, the benefits of those same medications needed to be weighed against the risks, since he was unable to metabolize medications effectively.

With my mind full of unanswered questions, I thought of the last euthanasia I had performed in conventional practice. A lovely, young chocolate Labrador came into our animal emergency clinic with his tongue five times its normal size. It was a stiff useless object holding his jaw open as though a giant piece of driftwood were stuck in his mouth, preventing him from eating or drinking. His person could barely afford the exam fee, much less other treatments or diagnostics. I pried the dog's mouth wide open to see the root of his problem. A deer's circular tracheal cartilage had tightly encircled the base of his tongue, constricting its blood flow. The dog must have wrapped the cartilage around his tongue while trying to ingest it. Hoping that removing the piece of cartilage would quickly fix the problem, I extracted the culprit with a pair of long forceps. To my dismay, the tongue remained unchanged. I told the dog's guardian that it might take time for the dog's swelling to resolve, but instead of taking him home and giving him a chance to heal, she requested euthanasia.

When I looked into his eyes, he appeared to know my intentions and made one last effort to move his tongue. I wondered if I would ever be able to forgive myself for what I was about to do. As I injected the euthanasia solution, I felt that I was betraying not only the dog, but myself too.

Most veterinarians accept the painful reality of euthanasia as part of their job, but that doesn't lessen the psychological impact. Fresh out of veterinary school, we new veterinarians were both uninformed and unprepared for our new job pressures and responsibilities, slowly discovering a stark reality to which we had not yet been hardened. My boyfriend at the time, David, painted his way out of depression.

Once he stayed up late, painting a picture of the handsome shepherd he had euthanized earlier that day, his private eulogy and coping mechanism. He knew he had done the right thing in quickly relieving the dog's suffering, but he struggled with the unsettled feeling of loss and the reminder of life's impermanence. I sensed David's deep sorrow with each stroke of his paintbrush, as though it had been me witnessing the guardian's profound sadness.

The finished painting revealed a beautiful canine portrait, the colors reflecting the light of a single life even though that life had now been extinguished. But even more than the dog's gold and black highlights, David had captured an expression of silent longing, singular to animals who know how to reach out to the kindness buried in all of us. "When are you giving that painting to the dog's owners?" I said, imagining how it might comfort them.

"Never," he whispered. After an initial phase of admiration, he placed the painting in the trash.

Is that why I worked so hard to save Jasper? Because I, myself, can no longer offer euthanasia? Tired of the unproductive chatter in my mind, I searched the trees for the answer. I looked out the tall windows from our yurt onto a temperamental sky, forgetting that nature does not judge. As I waited for an answer, shafts of light streamed through the clouds, the sun and rain mingling together. The sky laughed and cried. One eagle soared and another perched on top of a bent Douglas fir.

Dreaming of Horses

FOR YEARS, I WANTED a big Dutch warmblood horse, a breed revered for its acrobatic gaits of unearthly suspension and extension. In the summer of 2010, one of my clients decided to sell just such a horse. His name was Zeus, and since three other horsewomen were already interested in purchasing him, Jeff and I headed out early one Saturday morning to see him for ourselves. His reputation had spread throughout the horse community, if not for his handsome white blaze and four flashy socks, then for his natural talent to move forward and canter in small circles in the paddock. For an hour, Jeff and I drove through the peaceful countryside dotted with small farms.

"Donna, you deserve to have a talented horse. You've been

nursing Charlie's stifles for years," Jeff said. I thought of all my chiropractic adjustments and acupuncture treatments on Charlie's patellas and lumbar spine. Like most free horses from the racetrack, Charlie came as an expected lemon, having developed orthopedic problems at only three years old. It was understood that he was an old leaky clunker that would need oil every fifty miles. Early on, I had decided not to push him. My show days were long behind me.

When I was a kid, I begged mom for a fancy basset hound, the kind I saw in my *Encyclopedia of the Dog*. Mom, however, thought a purebred basset would be too expensive, so she picked up a long-backed mixed breed puppy at the shelter and gave her a fancy name, Julietta, hoping to appease me. Maybe today would be my chance to get the prized animal I'd dreamed about as a child, long before I related purebreds to disease susceptibility. We passed a row of perfect poplars by the side of the road. "He does sound nice. Who knows? Maybe we'll find a new friend for Charlie today," Jeff said.

As we drove along, I thought about horse-show mornings when I was young. Getting up before sunrise. The sweet smell of ShowSheen. The excitement at the prospect of blue ribbons and high score awards. There were so many loose ends before the show started: unraveled braids that didn't lay flat, green manure stains that needed to be removed and breeches that had to be scrubbed until they were so white that they glowed as bright as the sun rising over the horses when they loaded into the trailer.

During my show years, I also worked at the stable cleaning stalls, braiding horses' manes, and helping the veterinarian during his regular visits. One show morning when I was fourteen years old, my big chestnut, Bill, turned up lame, so we called old Doc Karl. Although I didn't know Dr. Karl's real age, he seemed a million years old to me that Saturday. Wrinkles weighed down his eyelids, either by years or fatigue or both. His hands had taken on a green tinge you could see through all his gnarled calluses. While most horse doctors deemed themselves experts, not just in veterinary medicine but in all subjects, we liked Doc Karl because he had the admirable ability to question his own judgment. He put his patients first, even, some said, to the detriment of his own marriage.

As he headed towards Bill's stall, he stopped to look at Buttercup, a palomino pony across the aisle, checking the thickness of her neck crest to see if she was gaining too much weight. A month earlier, Doc Karl had diagnosed Buttercup with laminitis, a painful and potentially deadly disease of the hoof, often seen in overweight ponies. "Gotta keep this old girl on a strict diet," he had grumbled, informing me that she could no longer be fed grain or even regular hay. Instead, her new hay resembled poor quality straw. I was told to put a sign on her door that read, "No Carrots, Please."

He then entered Bill's stall, felt all four digital pulses above each hoof and asked me to walk my big horse up and down the aisle. Even with his eyes closed, sitting on a hay bale with his back supported by the wall, Doc Karl could identify Bill's affected leg by the uneven sound of his footfalls against the concrete. "Left front," he said.

While he treated Bill's minor hoof abscess, I chimed in, "I want to go to vet school someday. Then I can find out why horses can't throw up. If they eat something poisonous, they're in big trouble," I said.

"That's why horses don't usually eat poisonous plants. They can smell the good from the bad," he said, holding the hoof between his knees. With a hoof knife that had seen sharper days, he carved into the sole of Bill's foot, looking for a dark red discoloration amidst the normal white tissue. He carefully dug for the cause of my horse's lameness using a sixth sense that can't be learned in vet school. As a pocket of pus and blood suddenly spurted up, he admitted that it had never actually occurred to him to wonder why horses do not vomit. Comfortable not knowing the answer, he smiled quietly and began soaking Bill's hoof in a bucket of antibacterial iodine solution that stained our fingers brown. He then packed the wound with medicated cotton.

Our conversation continued to hover around many ancient equine mysteries and strange diagnoses specific to horses. What causes stringhalt, sweeney, thoroughpin and proud flesh? And who came up with these names anyway? Although there would be no ribbons that day due to Bill's hoof abscess, I will always remember the quiet way our horse vet deftly treated Bill's ailments while, at the same time, he open-mindedly embraced what he did not know.

Jeff and I pulled up to the farm with its immaculate white picket fences and manicured indoor arena. And there he was. Zeus. He was impossible to miss, his head held high and proud. He was fully saddled and ready to go. We spoke to the farm manager for a while. "I have two other full-price offers. But if you want him, I'd practically give him to you," she said, appeasing the side of her that wanted the horse in a good home. In the high-rolling horse world, that translates to ten thousand dollars, but he'd be worth every penny. Jeff made small talk with Zeus's owner about the price of hay this year while I rode the majestic horse. It felt as though he actually grew ten inches as we extended into the trot, each stride covering seven feet, all of them off the ground. We cantered down the center line, starting with right lead flying into left, then left flying into right; each transition felt seamless and effortless.

He was an amazing horse, but I still wanted some time to think before committing to the purchase. Again, I thought about my show weekends while I was growing up. What I really missed most were the tiny details: the sound of my horse drinking, the rhythmic twitch of his ears with each gulp and the feel of his skin flicking off the fly as we lined up for ribbons. I began realizing that I didn't actually miss the ribbons themselves. As we were driving home, my cell phone rang with a call from animal control. They had just seized seven neglected horses in the next county. "Where are we going?" Jeff asked, as I hastily doubled back in the opposite direction.

"When I was looking at Zeus, something didn't quite feel right. Now I know what it was. With each animal we buy, another one remains homeless," I answered, deciding to follow my heart.

With a patience I had come to appreciate, Jeff sat silently beside me, having grown accustomed to my last minute changes of plans. Once again, I was giving into my terrier instincts. We pulled up to the holding paddocks and were immediately struck by the poor condition of the horses. Even though they had been fed a steady diet of hay for the last two weeks, the horses still looked extremely thin. An animal control officer met us by the gate and led us to the stronger, more dominant horses lined up near the front of the paddock. "These guys are the healthiest of the group," she said. But my only reaction was to look for which were the unhealthiest.

In spite of her words, or possibly because of them, I looked in the very rear of the paddock to see a small black horse. He stood alone under a cedar tree heaving for breath. "I doubt you want him. At least not yet. He was neglected the worst, and was so weak that he could barely lift himself out of the mud. He still has pneumonia and gets beat up on pretty good by the other horses." She wanted to spare us the grief, especially if his condition took a turn for the worse.

Like a homing pigeon, I walked across the manure-laden mud to the little horse. He stood frozen with fear. As I approached him, I immediately saw that his ribs and spine were protruding. On closer examination, I noticed scratches and patches of hair missing on his rump and legs. I opened his mouth expecting to find him "long in the tooth," Iris's expression for anyone her age or older. But instead, I saw the miniscule incisors of a young horse.

It wasn't his bald patches, scabs or elevated respiratory rate that grabbed me, but rather the way he hung his head in defeat, hiding behind a tree, hiding from an unfair life, hiding from everything and everyone. And somehow I knew that it was Smudge that had brought him to us, or us to him. Even in spirit, a terrier is determined and pushy. All at once, I remembered the first time I picked up the little black dog, armed with towels to clean up her urine. Her eyes had also blazed with fear. The small black horse was Smudge's double in a horse suit.

It would be a long journey to help him, as a horse's trust must be earned. It is not given away freely. The sun reddened his dark coat as he sniffed out the clover. I studied his large brown eyes. Although fearful, they were also kind. Without hesitation and with his lead rope already in the palm of my hand, I said, "I'll take him." The scruffy pony was in such a weakened state that he loaded into the trailer without any protest.

As we headed home, I felt that same sense of excitement that I always feel when adopting a new animal. "Okay, I know you already named him," Jeff said, smiling, "What are we going to call Charlie's new friend?"

I thought of how tiny he'd look next to Charlie who would tower almost three full hands above him. The word tiny stuck in my mind but that name might give him a complex. So I compromised. "I think I'll call him Tino."

Who Doctors Whom?

FIVE HOURS AFTER WENDY removed the Fentanyl patch from Jasper's rear leg, his attitude was already dramatically improving, his eagerness for life returning as he searched his bowl for dinner. It was clear that his listlessness and weakness could be attributed, at least that morning, to a side effect from his analgesic patch. By the next day, he was going on short walks. And by the weekend, he had planted himself stubbornly by the car, convincing Greg and Wendy to take him to the beach. Jasper scampered happily through the kelp and eel grass and dug in the sand, rooting for small crabs in a deep new hole he had excavated.

Two days after his near-death experience, Jasper returned to his nose work class, leaping up and down excitedly after discovering the small, birch-scented tin box hidden under an upside-down flowerpot. No one is more joyful than a golden retriever who has accomplished his mission. Nine weeks after his diagnosis, Jasper was once again bouncing all over the house at the thought of food or nose work.

Jasper's liver was the site of a constant battle between healthy cellular regeneration and the destructive effects of cancer with its associated reactive toxins. We were part of a dynamic physiologic struggle. My goal was to support his regenerative process while staving off as much damage as possible. For that reason, I chose a milk thistle, artichoke, dandelion leaf combination and fennel, four herbs that are very effective at healing and preserving healthy liver cells.

Wendy sat on the floor of my office with Jasper, trying to calm him down, while Greg marveled in disbelief at Jasper's renewed vitality. "How do we know which therapy is helping him?" Greg asked, his thin face taking on new optimism. Indeed, Jasper had significantly outlived our original predictions, now appearing quite healthy into his second month. But I also worried that his improvement might give the couple too much hope. Still, even though I knew sooner or later this cancer would probably win, I chose to stay as positive as possible.

"We can assume the supplements and herbs are helping Jasper

the most, but the acupuncture helps too," I said, thinking all the while about Jasper's strong life force despite his arthritis and cancer. "And the wonderful thing about acupuncture is that it also helps control his shoulder and back pain." We then spoke a while about the therapeutic qualities of the turkey tail and red reishi that I had prescribed for Jasper. I recommended occasionally replacing one medicinal mushroom with another. "Cancer can become resistant to herbs and other natural treatments after months of remission," I explained to Greg. "It's important to occasionally rotate Jasper's medications to help prevent that from happening."

"He sure feels good after his treatments," Greg said. As I watched the golden retriever licking Greg's face, apparently attempting to remove his mustache, I prepared my acupuncture needles. Carefully inserting each needle, I was once again amazed at how quickly Jasper relaxed into his treatment. In a few moments, he was almost asleep.

I explained the significance and benefits of each acupuncture point, tracing my finger along the liver meridian to signify the flow of qi along the channel. Every two weeks when I examined Jasper, I checked his pulse and tongue, and chose points based on his current symptoms, always needling Liver 3, the liver source point. Having finished my explanation, I looked up to see Greg's puzzled expression. He nodded the way I do when an auto mechanic explains that my CV boot needs replacing. Jasper patiently sat still for the customary fifteen or twenty minutes, looking like a large, long-haired pin cushion. Once I removed the needles, however, he immediately ran circles around all of us, licking our faces so fast that we had no time to retreat.

The main thing that impressed me was how the Millers *allowed* their dog to heal. In my mind, their openness to any effective but safe treatment encouraged the dog's remission. Although they may not have completely understood all of the subtle nuances of his therapy, they didn't obstruct Jasper's healing with negative doubts, or even worse, with excessive attachment to the outcome. Even though weeks passed in which Jasper's health improved, we still stuck to the notion that he may only live one more week. In this way, we applied no pressure to the dog. Jasper was an emotional sponge, able to sense and absorb a wide range of feelings and energetic imbalances. I often wished there was a device that could evaluate and quantify energy patterns and imbalances, such as Dr. McCoy's tricorder in *Star Trek*.

Years ago, the notion of these unproven and unquantifiable elements, so important in recapturing and maintaining health, drove my brother crazy. He would often attempt to disprove any belief of mine he did not share. We were both young and all-knowing, not yet weighed down by life's difficulties. But, unlike Neil, I was filled with an inner sense of mystery and beauty when I considered the world of the *unknown*. I was comfortable believing that I may never find answers to all my countless questions; in fact, I thrived on that childlike sense of wonder.

In the mid-nineties, during his break from graduate school at Harvard, Neil came with me to Sol Duc Hot Springs on Washington's Olympic peninsula, one of those tourist spots devoid of locals, but strangely full of Europeans. As we entered the crowded pools, I noticed towels strewn about on benches according to the chaotic law of entropy. Neil lowered himself into the warm water and I stepped in beside him. Steam swirled around us like a fog lifting from a stage, leaving the actors with no props to hide behind, only a backdrop of moss-covered trees.

A giant cedar shadowed Neil's face, which had grown older than mine, with small fissures along the outer margins of his eyes, remnants of work pressure and thesis deadlines. His hair grew prematurely grey and his skin dry, as though the large magnet in his laboratory had slowly drawn out and decanted all his youth. Although we typically carried at least five ongoing arguments, now with a growing audience of Germans and Austrians, we focused on just one. My brother believed with almost religious zeal that any disease process, any pattern of imbalance, could be explained on a cellular or genetic level.

So there we were, drunk with sulfur steam, yelling at one another over scientific notions of health. "You cannot tell if someone is yin or yang deficient by their chromosomes. That logic assumes that our health is determined solely by our genetics and nothing more," I said, standing on a cement step and holding the railing for support.

My opponent was not fazed. "Eventually we will know all possible variances and categorize them with genetic markers." A blond German in his fifties quietly applauded. Then Neil added, "*Sie ist ein Schmerz im Arsch.*" I hated it when he spoke in German, a language I could never even dream of deciphering. A small roar of laughter erupted from our audience.

Two kids knelt down for a splash fight.

"But what about the environment, the chemical triggers and radiation capable of turning genes on or off? What about the effects of all the carcinogens we encounter every day?" I could hear a faint grumble amidst some Austrians lined up in Neil's corner. My brother and I loved each other. We really did. But you couldn't tell when we hunkered down like seagulls fighting over a scrap of bread, all the while oblivious to the sting of our self-righteous opinions, unable to appreciate the grandeur of the rain forest.

He started in again. "It can all be genetically predicted. Even lysozymal enzymatic individuality will dictate which people will succumb to chemical triggers and which can overcome them." My world focused on the larger immune system, on finding ways to fortify a patient's inherent strengths. His world dissected a disease to its smallest core, its genetic sequence. We spun around and around, each so unfamiliar with the other's world, but so sure we knew it as well as our own.

When we were young, Neil would often grow irritated with me. "Donna, it's impossible to argue a point with you. Your logic darts around. It's not even as consistent as a circle; it's more like a Rorschach ink blot." When Neil presented an argument, he often did it in mathematical form, his favorite being the dot graph approach. Take any subject we'd commonly argue about, like whether every cancer was as individual as the person afflicted or if cancers could be classified using his molecular diagnostics, and he'd capture the nuance of the argument in a quantitative graphic, attempting to gain logical traction to support his side of the argument. Severity of disease on the y-axis, and molecular signatures on the x-axis. Then he'd decorate it with dots representing a patient population. His graphs rarely convinced me, but they sure looked impressive.

I recalled a phrase from a small book of Buddhist quotations: *People with opinions just go around bothering one another.* Now I could see the ridiculousness of it all, of arguing between science and holism, between the proven and the ethereal. Arguments so often trapped us into an egoist mindset of right and wrong, removing us from the work at hand, work we could only accomplish if we stayed in the present moment.

If there is one thing Jasper knew, it was how to *experience* the now of life. In the canine world of non-duality, a dog doesn't intellectually separate himself from those experiences—he *is* those experiences. When he drinks, he is the water. When he plays, he is the joy. If there is not enough water or food, he does not spend his day wishing for a reality that does not exist, as a human might. Instead he knows a world without psychological suffering, a world in which hours are not frittered away by wanting. Despite his cancerous liver and dwindling time on this earth, Jasper was easily the most enlightened being in our little exam room that morning.

There would be more near-death experiences and eventually, one day, we'd be forced to let go of Jasper's spirit, releasing it to find a new purpose. But for now, we all sat on a soft floor mat, watching sheets of mist slowly drift by outside the window. Because of Jasper's influence on us, we three humans were gradually changing. Greg's worry gave way to a thin smile. Wendy grew more confident in her intuition, and I felt honored to bask in Jasper's wonderful life force.

The sun filtered through the thick clouds of a February sky and lit up Jasper's white face, highlighting his bright butterscotch features. He was a dog on fire with life, his eyes eager to please, his nose forever twitching. I wondered if Jasper's mission was to heal us, instead of the other way around.

Trust Is Everything

WHEN TINO ARRIVED at our small farm, we immediately turned him out on the grass. Later, we taught him to pick up his feet and stand in the crossties. I treated the wounds behind his withers with one of Iris's strongest salves, an infused-oil mixture of comfrey root, calendula flowers and goldenseal root powder. Rubbing the pungent gel over his scabs became my morning routine. Unfortunately, all the close attention and medical treatments would often cause Tino to raise his head in alarm. It was obvious that he had never been cared for to any significant degree. But as one day's routine became another, his anxiety was soon replaced by boredom. His head began to drop down and his eyes started to close, opening only when an occasional gnat buzzed around his nostrils.

Once I finished with one wound, I'd notice another. I worked on each of his limbs in a clockwise fashion, so as not to overlook a scabby scar hidden in the shadow of his dull matted fur. I noticed small scabs on his ears, scars on his chest and a rope burn on his right rear leg, all evidence of a lifetime of neglect. At night I'd add warm water to his oats and after squishing the gruel between my fingers, I laced it with chia and hemp seeds, both rich in omega fatty acids. I also added a trace mineral powder, some lemon balm and passion flower powder to calm his frazzled emotional state. I was thankful that he ate the daily concoction, remembering that horses are walking stomachs, especially those with a history of starvation.

Routine daily events would often send Tino wildly lurching forward. A delivery truck driving up to the house. The sound of a dropped pitchfork hitting the ground. It seemed to take ages to blanket him at night, since every time I'd lift something over him, he'd lunge forward or step back. When he threw his head up, I knew he was no longer listening to me and it was time to give him a break.

But worst of all, his hooves had an uncanny magnetic attraction to my toes. No matter how quickly I'd move my feet, he would find a way to decorate the tops of them with round bruises, his daily parade atop my metatarsals. If a human tried to make mincemeat of my toes, I'd surely object, but since it was Tino, I scarcely noticed.

The minute one circular bruise turned yellow as it healed, a new green one quickly overshadowed it. Even with nightly applications of arnica gel, the tops of my feet looked like a mural of modern art.

Although his physical condition improved significantly over the next few months, Tino's coat taking on a vibrant reflective sheen like finely spun black silk, his mind and emotional state still suffered. The hours I spent on traditional ground work and lounging did little to serve us when conditions changed even slightly. During our afternoon walks down the gravel road, his eyes remained wide and cautious as our neighbors stopped to admire him, gazing at him with a childlike sense of awe. Even though my round-the-clock care was improving his health, his trust in my judgment remained thin.

Tino's thick mane now hung gracefully along his muscular neck and shoulders. His body was coal black with only ten white hairs on his forehead, invisible except by careful inspection. It wasn't his emerging beauty or his remarkably strong feet that captivated me. It was his gradual newfound desire to bond with other horses and humans. What he needed now were consistent rules and a leader he could trust. But, unaware of how to satisfy those needs, I just kept giving him love, the way a nurse tends to a wounded soldier. He would often nudge me softly as he tucked his head under my arm, his quiet attempt to communicate with me.

Years ago I learned that, even more important than medicine

or veterinary procedures, good training is what saves horses. So I received an abrupt lesson in humility when one day, a few months after riding him successfully with no problems, he bucked me off, a last-ditch attempt to communicate his unhappiness. Once the psychological sting of my fall dissipated, I formulated a list of excuses: the saddle did not fit, the mailman drove by, he heard a grouse in the brush, Venus was retrograde and the list went on. In reality, I just couldn't face the fact that he had rejected me. But a week later, when he bucked me off a second time, I was forced to face it.

Everyone wants to give away the horse that bucks you off, that scrapes you through the blackberries or dumps you in a nettle patch, but many horse people would gladly trade in a close family member rather than give up their trusted and dependable equine, the rare steed that will always carry you to safety.

Most of what I knew about horses came from years with trainers and riding instructors. Observing their old-school methods, I witnessed horses tied down with side reins, draw reins and miscellaneous ropes. These instructors also were fond of a process called desensitization in which an undesirable procedure, such as putting on a horse's halter, was repeated continuously until the horse finally learned to submit. The general idea being that if the horse resists something, we do it over and over again. Although they may have been successful at training horses for riding, showing and competitions, something was missing. They lacked the patience to build real trust.

I had used these old-school methods myself while training my own horses, both in England and New Jersey. I used a whip, not only as a directional tool, but to reinforce a gentle squeeze of my leg. In training young horses, I trotted them in tight circles in a round pen. Once they were exhausted, sweating and heaving, I considered them safe to ride. But no decision was ever made from the horse's own free will.

With Tino, there were indeed times when I needed to apply this philosophy. He appeared to feel crowded and trapped when caught between the fence and myself, but after repeating the apparently claustrophobic situation, he slowly began to realize that neither the fence nor I were dangerous. His discomfort in these situations told me that he had not made the decision that I was safe. He was still not bonded to me. As Tino walked freely through his paddock, I stood close by and carefully observed his body language. When I approached him, he turned his head away, his body freezing with just the pressure of my gaze.

In his book on healing human trauma, *Waking the Tiger*, Peter Levine describes freezing as the single most important factor in recovering from a traumatic experience. When Tino was confronted with fear, rather than striking or fleeing, he stood still, paralyzed. With fight-or-flight no longer an option, freezing had become my little horse's only coping mechanism. According to Levine, Tino was experiencing an evolutionary state in which he would feel no pain. It was as if he left his body, and although this altered state may have insulated him to some degree, from my point of view, it left him dangerously unpredictable.

Doubled over and gasping for breath after he bucked me off, I seriously wondered why I had adopted this horse. He stood looking at me from across the arena, his reins dragging in the sand. Even more than the growing pain that I felt in every bone in my body, I was struck by the incredible ease with which he had tossed me to the ground. "Do you have to ride him?" Jeff asked, as he applied my old standby, arnica salve, to my backside, massaging it in circles to treat the wide, rapidly forming bruises.

"Horses that are too dangerous to ride are the first to get euthanized, especially in this rough economy," I said, adjusting the ice pack over my tailbone. "If we were forced to find a home for him, he would be almost impossible to place since he would be considered dangerous." I had to find a way to transform him into a horse everyone wanted. After I stopped whining, I searched the Internet and found a unique rope-and halter-free way of training fearful horses, called Liberty Horse Training. Taking an action that some of my friends described as drastic, I flew to California to train one-on-one with Robin Gates in the Carolyn Resnick method of horse training. During my flight, I imagined Robin and myself dancing around the field with the horses.

The beautiful animals came to her as rescues, equines rejected by their previous owners who had deemed them untrainable. Although a few of the horses had been worth hundreds of thousands of dollars, their value had diminished drastically when they declined to sign up for the old, forceful training methods. Their stories varied widely. One show jumper shivered at the sight of a pole and refused to walk over it, despite the whips snapping behind him. Another dressage horse cringed at the notion of forced collection and a half-halt. Some of them had become dangerous, kicking or attacking the person who cared for them. Robin had gradually and miraculously changed them into the safest, most dedicated and connected of animals. She found beauty in each of their individual and spirited personalities. My only question was: how did she do it?

I spent the first afternoon observing Robin's techniques. What I witnessed was remarkable. As we drove along her fence line, she would call out the window to her horses, telling them to move to a different field, and to my amazement, all three raised their heads from the grass and obediently galloped away. Later that day, during another training exercise, one horse would stand on his back legs to get her attention and another would lie down at her feet, all four legs pointing horizontally as he gazed at her. And this was only the beginning.

Based on the herd dynamics of wild horses, Robin's training started with the idea of *who moves whom*. Instead of seeing humans as automatic candy dispensers, only there to freely dole out the treats, her horses learned that humans controlled specific, special food. And they had to earn it. The goodies, only given in small amounts, included apples, carrots and molasses-laden grain, the food horses really loved.

The next day, in an arena with a panoramic view of the arid Sonoma Mountains, Robin and her experienced bay gelding, Frankie, taught me my first lesson in Liberty Horse Training. Even though I was a British Horse Society certified assistant riding instructor, I found myself more than a bit lost in this new situation, on the ground with no reins, lead rope or even a halter to hold on to. Her face shaded by a long-brimmed hat, Robin called out instructions to me in a clear, strong and confident manner that I would come to admire. "Now, Frankie expects you to *show up*!"

The idea was easy to understand but deceptively complicated to orchestrate. Using minimal communication aids, most of which involved subtle body language, the goal was for the horse to *choose* to stay shoulder to shoulder with me as he mirrored my footsteps. I lightly tiptoed around, my thoughts drifting occasionally. Frankie immediately sensed my lack of decisiveness and began to wander away, leaving me standing alone with a puzzled look on my face in the middle of the sandy arena. I looked to Robin for help.

She marched up to me and said, "Donna, it's like this. You walk up to your husband and you say, 'Can I have a kiss?' But he only pecks you on the cheek and walks away. You were too vague, too indecisive and you were not really present. Why should Frankie listen to you when you, yourself, are lost in the clouds?" She barely stopped for breath, as passionate in her teachings as any master. "Now, what if you march up to your husband and say, 'I want a real kiss.' You demand it with your body and your whole being. You *demand* his connection with you. What kind of kiss will you get then?"

Robin proceeded to demonstrate the proper technique of Liberty Horse Training. She stood firmly with the balance and centeredness of a tai chi master. Frankie eagerly trotted up beside her. "Now, don't let Frankie push you," she continued. "Never move even the direction of your toes for a horse." I actually had to look down at my worn sneakers to determine the direction of my feet; I was that unaware of my body language.

I forced my all-too-busy mind to stay right there in the arena with Frankie. We walked side by side. When I jogged, he jogged. When I stopped and backed up, so did he. Small circles, wide turns, and weaving in between bright orange cones. We were creating a bond. At times, he almost appeared to be reading my thoughts. Robin told me that, in Liberty Horse Training, the horse's attention should be solely on you. And if he is truly in the *bond*, you can move your left shoulder forward and your right shoulder back and he will mirror that movement. In essence, you move him with only a small directional change of your toes and shoulders. It's like dancing with an equine partner. And it began to feel completely natural.

Moving from horse to horse, I realized that each one had his own personality and was encouraged to express his opinion. One decided to show me his repertoire of tricks, rearing up on his hind legs and then kicking out as though performing in the famous Spanish school for horse acrobatics. Another horse, apparently unsure of my commitment, would only look at me with one eye, forcing me to patiently strengthen my presence until he squared to face me. The last one ignored me entirely until I silently stood nose to nose with him, allowing him to bond with me on his own terms.

One of the most useful tools I learned during the week was an exercise called *the draw*. Robin would instruct me to send away or release the horse, suggesting that he now had the freedom to race around the arena without any restrictions. Then a moment later, I would ask him to come back to me, requesting that he immediately return to a calm state. I repeated this over and over until it seemed natural. Robin explained the value of this exercise: if a horse became fearful and bucked his rider off on a trail ride, rather than race back to the barn as most horses would do, he would immediately return to his rider.

I had mixed feelings about my upcoming Liberty Horse Training session with Tino. Up to this point, I had only worked with horses that had already been schooled in this method. So Tino, having no previous training, might pose a significant challenge. Attempting to console myself, I recalled that some of these horses I had worked with over the last week had actually tried to injure their owners, sometimes succeeding. Tino had never kicked me, chased me down or trampled me, so I figured that we were pretty much halfway there. I headed home with a new sense of optimism.

Returning to our farm, I filled Tino's hay bins and placed a tub of sweet carrots in the middle of his large paddock. While giving him plenty of space to retreat from me if he felt fearful or confused, as well as giving him free access to his hay, I prevented him from approaching the carrots. Apparently shocked at my control over his special food, he snorted loudly in protest. I was obviously communicating with him, and even better yet, in his own language.

My next hurdle was to teach him that in order to receive the carrots, he had to work for them. Over the next hour, I was able to convince him that if he walked a few steps with me, he would receive a piece of carrot. A few more steps, another piece of carrot or a gentle scratch along his itchy neck.

But as he walked by my side, he still harbored a degree

of nervousness. I then jumped towards him, waving my arms, encouraging him to run freely around his paddock, with the assumption that I could easily bring him back in a few moments. But instead he galloped into his shed and refused to approach me again. Having used too much force to send him away, I remembered that occasional failures were going to be part of the learning process.

Years ago, I would have marched into that shed with his halter and lead rope in hand, bringing him back whether he liked it or not. But in my new style of training, I needed to let him make his own decisions. Forcefully going in after him would have taught him nothing. There was only one choice. I had to sit in the middle of his paddock, a bucket full of carrots at my feet, and wait. The minutes and hours slowly passed. I crunched on a carrot. Jeff brought me a drink. When it rained, he brought me an umbrella. He canceled our plans for the night. When it grew colder, he brought me a coat. He said nothing because he knew Tino and I stood at a training crossroads.

Every few minutes, Tino nervously looked in my direction, but then shook his head, turned away from me and stubbornly stood his ground. At that point, it wouldn't have mattered if I had a dozen Red Delicious apples. Tino had reverted to that frozen immobile state that, to him, meant survival. It was all he could trust. And trust is everything in the horse world.

The Diagnosis

I WAS LEARNING FROM Tino to focus on the larger picture instead of on one specific problem. But even after all this time, I had trouble applying that lesson to Jasper's cancer. For six months, the Millers and I had kept Jasper alive in relatively good health by directing our treatment towards his immune system and protecting his undamaged liver cells, fostering an environment for their rapid regeneration. But as I talked to colleagues about Jasper and thought about his progress, my focus strayed from his liver and immune system to those tumors. Were they malignant after all? Had they shrunk? Were they still pressing on the vena cava? I wanted other veterinarians to know about the holistic options for cancer therapy, especially in older patients. Without a liver biopsy, though, I knew they would question the diagnosis, and Jasper's apparent recovery.

Despite my internal struggle, during his next appointment, we all beamed with appreciation for life, especially Jasper. We laughed as he ran to the treat counter, back to the herbal pharmacy, up to Wendy and Greg, and then to all points in between. The dog was now overweight! Because Jasper seemed even healthier now than before his presumptive diagnosis, I began to wonder if those tumors had decreased in size or, better yet, disappeared altogether.

My acupuncture treatments had been tailored to Jasper's symptoms, pulses and the quality of his tongue. If his pulses felt wiry, I'd needle points to bring the dog's energy deeper to his core, and alleviate stagnation in his meridians. If his pulses felt normal, I'd use fewer needles, still focusing on the liver source point located on the inside of both hind legs, an ancient point known to keep the liver resilient, nourished, and adaptable. I equated his tumors to leaky water balloons. The more they filled with water, the more they leaked their damaging fluid. I did not want to fill those balloons—I wanted to relieve their inner pressure. Since some acupuncture points opened the faucet, I avoided them, choosing other points that would turn it off.

At one point, following my suggestion, the Millers tried an acupuncturist closer to their home. She needled acupuncture points directly above the tumors, points that opened the faucet to stimulate hepatic circulation, and subsequently, Jasper suffered another minor bleeding episode. Likewise, giving Jasper any supplement that promoted liver circulation, including alpha-lipoic acid or red clover tea, resulted in a number of adverse side effects.

Much of Jasper's therapy also revolved around detoxification, so we added green tea extract, bioflavonoids and burdock root to his already specially formulated raw diet. At one point, Wendy was administering over fifty pills and capsules a day to Jasper, not including his powdered herbal preparations. But he happily took to these healthy medicines, regarding them as routine.

"Would you consider repeating Jasper's ultrasound?" I asked Wendy, motivated by my desire for a definitive histopathologic diagnosis. "I think it would be helpful to have a current picture of his tumors." Like most of my more traditional colleagues, I felt that a concrete diagnosis would help me stand on solid ground. But I also knew that since Jasper was responding so well to his treatment, an unequivocal pathology report would help bolster the validity of my style of medicine. Forgetting Iris's lesson about being humble, I found my ego getting in the way of my decisions.

It was clear that Wendy questioned my new approach. "Why repeat the ultrasound when he is doing so well?" She stroked Jasper's forehead as the acupuncture needles strengthened their usual meridians. Greg also looked confused. After all, since visits with the conventional veterinarian caused Jasper to fearfully tremble from head to tail, a repeat visit for an ultrasound might compromise his delicate health.

"Well, it might affect Donna's choice of herbal treatments," Wendy said, sounding unsure of herself. Greg shrugged. I didn't expect them to follow up on my recommendations, but two days later, I was surprised to find out that the Millers had decided to take Jasper for further testing.

At Dr. Roberts's clinic, they drew Jasper's blood sample and performed the ultrasound, but wisely decided against a biopsy, judging the process to be far too risky. Any routine procedure stressed the dog so much, even a benign ultrasound was life-threatening because Jasper's health was so fragile. Unfortunately, after the imaging study, the dog's gums became pale, indicating that his tumors had once again begun to bleed. The only discovery made during the procedure was a let-down for all of us hoping for regression in tumor size: the ultrasound findings revealed that the tumor remained unchanged.

Wendy called me later that afternoon and reported Jasper's worsening condition. We all felt guilty, especially me. Jasper, a relatively healthy dog only two days ago, now remained hospitalized, with intravenous fluids maintaining his blood pressure. Due to his unstable condition, taking him home was not an option. Wendy brought him homemade food, which he refused, and a basket of toys. Jasper immediately chose the one item that he cherished the most, one of Greg's dirty socks. This specific sock had also comforted Jasper in the past when Greg had to spend a month in the human hospital. Jasper took the sock into the back of his cage, tucking it under his belly as though it were his own private treasure.

After giving Jasper extra doses of Yunnan pao yao and homeopathic *Phosphorus* according to my directions, Wendy waited in the hospital lobby, quietly working on her cross-stitching. Later, when she could barely keep her eyes open, she drove home. As she crawled into bed, she put the phone on her pillow, in the very spot where Jasper's head had rested the night before. I stayed up late pacing around the house, silently apologizing to myself for going against my highest ideals. I felt as though I had violated some ancient contract between healer and patient.

"Recommending that ultrasound was not the wrong thing to do," Jeff said as we lay in bed, his voice startling me in the darkness. "Any other veterinarian would have done the same thing. Ultrasound is one of the safest and most valuable tools that we have." He put his hand on my shoulder, consoling me as though Jasper had already passed away.

"But we take an oath to do no harm, and I feel like I violated it today," I said, shifting in bed. "I should have known that the stress might push him over the edge." The rain pitter-pattered on the roof. The sound was a reminder that we are part of nature, interconnected and bound by a common energy. But I was too busy beating myself up to hear the rain's message.

On that restless night, I thought about Doc Karl. A thirteen-year-old budding animal doctor, I stood in my horse's stall waiting for the old veterinarian to begin working on my horse's sore hoof. With icy ungloved hands, I held a clean bandage and my horse's lead rope while squaring a bucket of warm water between my ankles. I could see that Doc Karl was haunted by the fear of losing his patient, a mark of a doctor who cared too much. On cold late nights, Doc Karl would often attempt to discourage me from being a veterinarian, but somehow his comments had the opposite effect. Describing his equine patients as "a species bent on its own self-destruction," he said, "They'll follow you home and into your dreams. That is, if you are lucky enough to sleep at all."

Above All, Do No Harm

AFTER GRADUATING FROM VETERINARY school, I worked in a large ten-doctor referral center just outside Chicago. The clinic took up the better part of a city block and was a throwback to the 1950s, with its peeling green paint and rectangular blue sign, barely visible at night with only a single bulb partially illuminating it from below. Within a few months, a national corporation would buy up the clinic and replace our rickety wood sign with a giant red neon one, but I didn't know that yet. I liked the way it felt when I walked through the squeaky front door. I liked that it was old and worn, like a pair of jeans that had been stitched back together over and over again.

The senior veterinarian was an ex-Navy guy who did not

subscribe to the values of a newer generation. He did not read *Veterinary Economics*, a magazine created because of people like him, old characters who didn't know how to charge enough money. Clients only paid ten dollars for an exam, a fee waived with annual vaccines. Expressing anal glands, cleaning ears and trimming nails were free before corporate interests began charging for every last cotton ball. If we could efficiently treat a patient and charge very little, we were congratulated at staff meetings. I would often see forty patients on a slow day. I recall treating a black cat's frostbite, a spaniel's heartworm disease, and a severe case of ear mites in a tiny kitten all within one hour. I remember peering in the microscope, mesmerized as my first mite flailed its tiny legs under oil immersion.

My goal during that first year was to learn when to use conventional medicine (when its benefits outweighed the risks) and when to use holistic therapies. After working all day, I'd lay awake at night, with Smudge curled up by my side, thinking of Iris and her miraculous herbal treatments. I remembered how Sampson's red, open sores gave way to new skin, then peach fuzz, and finally, a thick, full poodle coat.

My colleagues, leery of holistic medicine, encouraged me to stick to conventional therapies. So for now, I was limited to medications that began with the prefix *anti*. I prescribed antibiotics, antihistamines and anti-inflammatories.

And I marveled at some of my successes using conventional medicine. That cat with nasal mites, his sneezing cured with a single injection of ivermectin. Another cat with an abscess and high fever, whose signs improved dramatically after only a day of antibiotics. Although not a big fan of the surgical suite, I found myself gloving up and performing Caesarian sections, delivering a litter of puppies in the wee hours of the morning. Surgery was rewarding when it went well. Our surgeon's motto hung over his desk: *A chance to cut is a chance to cure.*

But I began to think more carefully about that motto and wondered if it really held true for all patients. Procedures that were safe for young healthy animals might prove fatal when performed on old, frail patients. I began to wonder if the feeblest of all patients might be better off with no treatment, rather than suffer the risks of surgery. When an older dog ruptured an intervertebral disc, rather than recommending surgery for his spinal condition, I found myself searching for safer treatment options. I then recalled another age-old surgeon's motto, one that did not hang above the surgeon's desk: *The surgery was a success, but the patient died.* The surgeons often laughed at this phrase. But with a sobbing client on the other end of the phone, I failed to see the humor in it.

It was not surgery, alone, that had a dark side. Medications had created a rollercoaster of side effects for one of our patients, a loveable Labrador mix named Sheeba. Receptionists, who only left the confines of their desks for donuts, always got up to pet her. The technicians had given her a special nickname, Mellow Yellow. But whenever I saw her name on my daily schedule, I worried about what new symptoms we might have created.

At twelve years old, Sheeba's life revolved around her daily medication schedule, a list of drugs that seemed to grow by the day. We had tried multiple anti-inflammatories for her arthritis, which resulted in gastritis and liver disease. To alleviate these side effects, we prescribed anti-emetics and hepatoprotectants. Add to the list anti-ulcer medications and antacids, and what started off as one arthritis medication had snowballed into a long list of current pharmaceutical drugs. These drugs took a significant financial toll on Sheeba's human, Mr. Sawyer, an older man on a fixed income. Some of my colleagues might have been inclined to add even more medicines while I was inclined to subtract. Eventually, Sheeba died due to a perforated gastrointestinal ulcer, one of the most serious potential side effects of non-steroidal anti-inflammatory medications.

The morning I found out about Sheeba's death, I felt sadness and regret about the management of her health. Working through a dense fog of uncertainty, I slowly and methodically performed each of my daily tasks: taking a dog's temperature, incising a dog's abdomen for her routine spay and threading a tiny intravenous catheter in a cat's vein. At one point, I stood frozen in our large pharmacy staring mindlessly at the medications before me. These clean, white, neatly stacked bottles governed the future of our patients. Would these medicines cure disease or create disease? I was only one person standing to face an insurmountable industry, one that had grown too large and uncontrolled to remain safe.

On the heels of the lesson I learned from Sheeba, perhaps my biggest moral dilemma came in a much smaller package. I first examined Mary Ann when she was fourteen years old. She was a small calico cat, seven pounds tops, with the greenest eyes I had ever seen in a feline and lynx-like black tufts sprouting from her ears. Her caretaker was a stern matronly woman who resembled the kind of librarian unlikely to tolerate overdue books. Her name was Mrs. Mallet and just the sight of her in the lobby sent the other veterinarians scattering to all corners of the hospital. During our appointments, her eyes squinted with fierce intensity as she grilled me for answers to her questions.

During one particular appointment, Mary Ann had licked at a small sore on her right front foot. I insisted that the wound would heal with a topical antibiotic ointment and that it was likely caused by a scratch from another cat. Mrs. Mallet, however, pressed me until I created an exhaustive list of unusual, but possible, diagnoses, from ringworm to skin cancer to a rare autoimmune eosinophilic plaque. Mrs. Mallet just wanted to prepare for the worst. When she left with her list of every known feline disease, I needed time to recover before seeing another client.

But if an animal were in need, Mrs. Mallet would immediately rally to its aid. Whether it was rescuing and neutering stray cats, helping pay bills for low-income clients or stopping by the side of the road to check a dead possum's pouch for surviving babies, Mrs. Mallet always put the animals first.

One hot summer afternoon, she brought us a panting, dehydrated pit bull with heatstroke. "I pulled this one from a minivan in the mall parking lot," she said, practically panting herself as she helped carry his stretcher into the back treatment room. As we quickly placed an intravenous catheter and began administering fluids, she proudly displayed her trusty spring-loaded center punch, a tool she had placed tight up in the corner of the car's side window to break the glass, retrieving the dog by his armpits. "Idiots," she added, referring to the people who had left their dog in the car. "Another minute and that dog would have died."

Because Mrs. Mallet had been so diligent about Mary Ann's annual examinations, we had diagnosed a heart murmur in its early stages five years ago. This early diagnosis, along with proper medication, added years to the cat's life. But as she grew older and more frail, her routine veterinary visits gradually became more stressful. Now at fifteen years old, with her hearing and eyesight failing, I was unable to accurately evaluate her heart condition due to her constant panting and trembling. Even brief examinations began to seem detrimental to her health.

Although Mrs. Mallet's horned-rimmed, black-framed glasses and beady eyes gave her an intimidating appearance, a bright yellow silk scarf tied neatly and snugly around her neck lightened her demeanor. And when she explained things to Mary Ann, her gruff tone softened as if speaking to a child. "Mary Ann, Dr. Kelleher is trying to help you. She needs to listen to your heart." She lifted the elderly kitty onto the exam table. But the small cat's severe panting made it extremely difficult to hear her lungs and heart. "How long do you think she has to live?" she asked me, with a faint trace of fear in her voice. Her questions were always direct, carved from stone and lacking the softness reserved only for her cat.

I explained that Mary Ann's failing heart was probably causing fluid to back up into her lungs, leading to a condition called congestive heart failure, a label that lacked the diplomacy and compassion so desperately needed when clients are receiving such dire news. Had the word "failure" been associated with Mary Ann's kidneys, given proper treatment and a little luck, she still might have years to live. But in this case, failure meant *failure*. I predicted that Mary Ann may have weeks, rather than months, to live.

Over the next month, Mary Ann's health deteriorated to the

degree that even the shortest appointments would cause labored respiration, although her breathing was normal at home. No matter how insignificant we humans deemed it, the stress of a brief office visit finally drove Mary Ann into an open-mouth pant one day, prompting me to put her into an oxygen chamber and beg Mrs. Mallet not to bring her in anymore.

Mary Ann reminded me that something as seemingly benign as a routine examination could have life-threatening complications. I remembered an anxious toy poodle scheduled for a routine blood draw and urinalysis. After we finished his procedure and returned him to his human, anxiety and fear still lingered in the exasperated dog's eyes. I turned to leave, and when the poodle's person thought no one was listening, I heard her quietly apologize to her small companion: "I'm sorry. I promise, no more vet visits."

I did not want Mrs. Mallet to have to say those words to Mary Ann. While I would have preferred to monitor her heart condition closely, her stress level made that impractical. I knew that my coworkers might not have made the same decision, but I had to live with myself. It was safer to do things Mary Ann's way. She lived another year and died in her sleep one night, outliving any of our predictions.

When I considered Jasper's precarious health, I recalled Sheeba, Mary Ann and the lessons I had learned and needed to relearn. It reminded me of a well-known veterinary professor who started the

Urolith Analysis Center at the University of Minnesota in 1981. The center analyzed bladder stones, free of charge, in exchange for vital dietary information on each patient, hoping to reduce the need for unnecessary surgery. The professor discovered that many of these painful stones had a dietary basis, and that urolithiasis could be prevented, not by pharmaceutical intervention, but with specific and individualized diet recommendations—a novel concept for that time. He conveyed *primum non nocere* to his veterinary students when he said, "There are some animals we cannot help, but there are none we cannot harm."

Connecting with a Horse

TINO LOOKED OUT from the safety of his shed, worried about only one thing. Me. And more specifically, my expectations. Determined not to chase him down with a halter, I sat fifty feet away from him with a bucket of carrots by my side. I waited for him to come out on his own, occasionally calling his name and presenting a carrot in my palm.

Tino was teaching me two cardinal rules of horse language, those of fairness and effective, consistent leadership. In his mind, by strongly sending him away with large arm movements, I had violated both. During my fourteen years with Charlie, an extremely dominant horse, I had become accustomed to using a loud voice, big commands and, if needed, a snap of the whip in order to communicate my wishes. Anything less would have been ignored. But Tino was the opposite. While often I needed to yell at Charlie, Tino wanted me to speak in a whisper. In a wild horse herd, the leader will communicate only what is necessary to each horse, no more and no less. This amount of communication varies depending on the submissive horse's individual personality and sensitivity. My challenge now was to become a skillful and consistent leader, but remain just, fair and kind.

Huddled in a frightened, tense stance towards the back of his shed, Tino shook his head and pinned his ears back. I recalled an interesting concept offered by Magali Delgado and Frédéric Pignon, the brilliant founders of *Cavalia*, an inspiring performance of Cirque du Soleil that includes elements of Liberty Horse Training. In their book, *Gallop to Freedom*, they provide a unique insight into horse-human communication: "Misunderstanding between horse and human produces an even greater barrier between them than ill treatment." Truly there was a misunderstanding between Tino and me, and it had indeed created a barrier between us. But Megali and Frédéric offered the following hopeful conclusion: "Understanding will, on the other hand, begin to forge a link between horse and human." My only question now was how could I create an understanding between the two of us? The answer seemed just out of reach.

Their message was akin to the philosophy of holistic medicine.

My conventional medical training had always focused on pathology or disease, just as the old-style horse training focused on negative behavior. But in holistic medicine, I fostered overall wellness through strengthening the entire body's immune, endocrine and organ systems. Similarly, Liberty Horse Training emphasized the whole horse by creating a trusting bond, mutual understanding and a foundation of positive thought.

Attempting to see the world through a horse's eyes, I realized that sitting motionless in one place might be considered predatory behavior, a tiger patiently stalking its prey. So I gradually stood and began wandering in small circles, looking up at the clouds, listening to the birds and creating a peaceful place inside myself in which I did not expect anything from him. I relaxed my body and dropped my shoulders to appear smaller. I focused on my breathing, concentrating on long, slow, deep breaths, a moving meditation. When Tino took one step towards me, I quietly said, "Good boy," establishing eye contact only when he looked up at me. And if he retreated a step, I would retreat too, gently matching his energy.

I recalled my old meditation instructor, who had once given a preparatory talk before sitting silently for a whole day. "The body mirrors the mind. If your mind is unsettled, your body will be restless. But if you allow your thoughts to pass through your mind like clouds in a blue sky, eventually, your mind will become clear." As I sat watching Tino, I noticed the clouds floating by. A graceful heron silently glided above us. At that moment, Tino began cautiously walking towards me, pausing occasionally, as though he doubted his growing trust in me, but nonetheless overcoming his uncertainty with each step. Eventually he stood beside me. Careful not to make any sudden movements, I slowly handed him some grain and scratched his withers until he was sure that all I wanted was companionship. The focus had shifted from coercion to cooperation, from eliminating a negative behavior to fostering a bond.

When I turned to walk away, he chose to walk with me. He had decided that being emotionally connected to me felt better than wandering away on his own. So, I opened the gate and we walked together around the field. Once in a while I bent to show him grass, telling him with silent body language, "Now is a safe time to eat." After a few minutes, he'd walk beside me again, chewing and lowering his head as he relaxed. If I turned my shoulders slightly, he mirrored my action. Before long, we were trotting together, occasionally halting and backing up with no verbal cues, only gentle body language and close attention to the present moment.

As the weeks passed, Tino's confidence grew and he began seeking me out over the gate, whinnying his enthusiasm for whatever I had lined up that day. Some days I'd set up an obstacle course with small poles, a green mounting block and a purple exercise ball. I would allow him to discover his own games:

grabbing the ball with his teeth and tossing it in my direction or flinging an empty burlap sack into the air. After hiding treats under rocks or upside-down tubs, I'd watch him and laugh as he happily discovered them one by one.

Over the next few months, I would have to repeatedly apply the ideas of trust and acceptance as Tino and I forged our new relationship. It was a sunny day in March when a small group of horsewomen joined me for a ride up a steep slippery trail behind our house. Even with no certain breeding history or known lineage, Tino could have run circles around all the other horses, most of them expensive warmbloods that were more at home in a dressage arena than on a narrow trail. As they tripped over logs and clumsily lurched their heavy bodies up the trail, Tino used his hooves like hands, gripping each step with the dexterity of a mountain goat. While his ears listened to my cues, he tapped into his own deep reservoir of new confidence.

"Donna, where did you get that talented little horse?" one woman said, already breathless from her own horse's anxiety, an emotion carried through to her.

Going into Tino's full story would bring back too many negative shadows of the past. I thought of the scars, wounds and hours of working with him at Liberty. "I just found him in a muddy paddock," I replied. I gave him a pat and we passed up the big horses, slowly climbing towards the clear blue sky.

A Dog's Choice

JASPER HAD NOW SPENT the last two days in the hospital on intravenous fluids and was showing minimal signs of improvement. Dr. Roberts remained skeptical about his ability to recover. After all, Jasper was a dog with cancer, and that was not about to change. Having gone from eating over a pound of raw and cooked food only three days ago, Jasper now refused even the most tempting treats. In order to regain his energy, he would have to regain his appetite. Greg and Wendy sadly peered at Jasper's row of untouched steel bowls.

In veterinary school, we learned that weight loss and lack of appetite were two of the hallmark signs of cancer. Believing that the cancer had spread, Dr. Roberts called me to report on

Jasper's current condition. But this time, she wasn't mentioning euthanasia.

"Have you tried B-vitamin injections or baby food?" I asked Dr. Roberts over the phone, all the while knowing she was aware of all the tricks to keep a dog interested in eating.

"Yes. We've corrected his anemia, but we still can't get him to eat. I don't know if the problem is his declining liver function or the cancer itself," she said. "We can always try corticosteroids." I was reluctant to use prednisone unless there was absolutely nothing else we could do. Its potential side effects included muscle wasting, cartilage breakdown and liver problems, and although it would likely stimulate Jasper's appetite, the risks might outweigh the benefits.

Once again, our list of options was limited, and I realized that in order to help Jasper, I needed to look at his illness in a different way. I began to think about Tino and his path to recovery. Just as I had to move from the old-school training methods to a more holistic training approach, I now had to shift from concentrating on Jasper's tumors to addressing his overall wellbeing; in both cases, I was moving from a focus on the negative to a focus on the positive. At that point, it seemed that Wendy had read my mind and she came up with a better idea.

She decided that, rather than forcing food upon him, she

would create a game. If Jasper was unable to go to nose work class, the ever-determined Wendy would bring the class to him. Greg and Dr. Roberts agreed to try her plan, as far-fetched as it seemed. So, in the middle of the busy clinic, with a cat hissing from an upper level cage and a sick Jack Russell terrier watching the commotion, Wendy clicked open Jasper's steel cage door. Greg dutifully wheeled the IV stand wherever his dog took him. With an intravenous catheter and a thick red bandage still in place on Jasper's front leg, he meandered with Wendy and Greg across the room until the three of them stood in the middle of the treatment area, fluids still dripping into his bloodstream.

She took an open cardboard box, turned it over and placed the scented tin container beneath it. "Come on, Jasper," she said. "Go find it." The old golden retriever looked up with a surprised expression as everyone watched: two technicians, the veterinarian, and even the kennel cleaner in the back. For a breathless moment, Jasper showed no interest in the game. But Wendy remained steadfast in her playful, expectant command, repeating it several times. Jasper remained motionless, as if he stood at a crossroads between engaging in or withdrawing from life, a decision that everyone, animal or human, makes every moment. Every moment is a choice.

Jasper sat down beside his family, the plastic tubing of his IV line draped between them. Wendy repeated her command. "Go find it!" she said. His nose then began to twitch with a newfound spark of life. In a few moments, it spread to his eyes and then to his tail, and then to each person in the room as he looked up at everyone. Ignoring his bandage, plastic tubes, and Greg who was awkwardly perched above him, he walked over to the box and barked with new energy. Wendy quickly offered him a bowl of boiled turkey and pumpkin, rubbing him down along his sides and ruffling his long coat against its grain, playfully pleading for Jasper to eat. He sniffed at the food as his humans held their breath. And then, to everyone's amazement, Jasper began to eat, gaining enthusiasm with each bite, until he had finally licked his bowl clean. A wave of excitement swept over his small audience, especially Greg and Wendy.

Jasper's appetite was renewed by the power of his fearless seeking instinct. During the previous two days in his cold sterile cage, Jasper had lost his will to live. And nose work had helped him find his own initiative in life, a force more powerful than any medicine.

Now in his sixteenth month of remission, Jasper still runs into my clinic, a dog that knows how to smile. Other clients see him in the parking lot or in the waiting room, and are forced to forget their problems. They smile, too, at the golden retriever on a mission to spread happiness.

The Tree of Life

SMUDGE HAD BEEN my constant companion for many years. Although she was considerably slower-moving in her later years, the adventures towards the end of her life were no less important than those rambunctious ones over a decade earlier. At sixteen years of age, still thriving and free of cancer, she continued to accompany us on short hikes in the woods.

But during the summer of 2007, she began showing some early neurological signs, slowly rocking back and forth. One day, she stared at me for several minutes, her eyes glued to mine. Now I wish I had stopped everything at that moment so I could say goodbye to the lively Smudge I had always known. It was the last day before blindness overtook her, leaving her in a world of shadows.

Because Smudge's ophthalmologic exam was essentially normal, we were met with the gloomy realization that her blindness was likely due to a brain lesion, since it's the brain that sees and not the eyes. This also meant that little could be done to help her. To support her neurologic function, I added more B vitamins, folate, coenzyme Q10 and glutathione to her diet, all the while knowing that my remedies might have a limited effect. On the one hand, I accepted the natural process of Smudge's aging, and on the other, I fell into despair.

Jeff built two wooden square enclosures, one for inside the house and one for outside, to prevent her from wandering off or getting stuck in a corner. Within those enclosures, Smudge took herself on daily walks, always circling to the right. She continued to eat ravenously and raised her head when we entered her room, as hearing had become her best sense. I would cradle her on her back as she stared past me, into her own world.

Smudge also began an unfortunate hobby of finger-painting with her paws. After venturing off her pillow to defecate, rather than leaving an inartistic, untouched pile for us, she would circle through it, over and over again, until it was ground into the cement floor. The radiant heat system then caused the smell to permeate every room in the house. Jeff and I spent many mornings on our hands and knees, scrubbing vigorously to remove Smudge's own form of brown mosaic art. Then one day, a client with a paralyzed dog gave me a washable doggie diaper with Velcro fasteners along the hips. Because it contained a pouch under the tail hole, the diaper worked magically for our situation. We bought ten of them, five navy blue and five forest green.

Between the towels and diapers, the washing machine in our barn received a daily workout. I hung her diapers on the fence to dry in the sun, the tail holes lining up neatly in a row. We carried her outside six or seven times a day, her bladder and colon working overtime. This did not include the middle-of-the-night trips, complete with a flashlight. And this was our routine for two years. I included Smudge in my daily activities and limited my work hours, tucking her under my arm when I talked to clients on the phone.

But one night, as she was wandering in circles, she suddenly cried out and became extremely restless. Trying every acupuncture and chiropractic technique I had ever learned, I was unable to alleviate her discomfort. After two doses of valium did not settle her nerves, and morphine caused her even more anxiety, I agonized over what to do next. Having long been a supporter of the animal hospice movement, I had always hoped she would die in her sleep. Helplessly crouching next to her as she whined on her pillow, I gently touched her forehead. Reluctantly, I asked Jeff to euthanize her.

"Are you sure?" he asked me, having never known me

without her.

Tears welled up—in my eyes, in my lips and in the back of my throat. I wanted to be brave for Smudge, but knew that I did not possess even half her courage.

I held her on her back as I did when I brushed her teeth. I looked into her eyes, trying to find a remnant of connection in her distant gaze. I imagined borrowing her courage in order to stay strong. After Jeff had injected only a quarter of the dose of the euthanasia solution, she quietly left her body. Although her vision had been clouded for many years, her eyes now seemed to gaze with a new clarity, past her square enclosure, past our yurt and forest and towards some distant place I could only imagine. Though in constant motion in her younger years, her body now grew still and cold. Her tongue, which once so eagerly explored our world, became constricted, all color erased like a black and white photograph.

Gently and respectfully, Jeff crossed her front paws beneath her head and closed her eyes. In a soft monotone voice, he chanted the heart sutra, first in Korean, and then in English.

"Ma-ha ban-ya ba-ra-mil-ta shim gyong . . . No ignorance and no end of ignorance, no old age and death and no end of them. No suffering, no craving, no extinction, no path, no wisdom, no attainment with nothing to attain. The Bodhisattva relies on Prajna Paramita

with no hindrance in the mind. Without any hindrance no fears exist. Far beyond every delusion, one dwells in Nirvana."

Stunned and lost, I realized that I was not fully prepared to let my best friend go. I sat with her body all night, clipping a few long hairs from the tip of her tail. After a while, I came to see that the body I knew as Smudge only acted as a shell, now outgrown by her great spirit. I tried to reach out beyond that shell into a universal light, a universal force, but as hard as I tried, in that dark room, I couldn't find her.

I took her body back to the woods, tucking it under my chest as I gazed in disbelief at her motionless face. Silence surrounded us in the early blue light of the morning, a stillness broken only by the sound of a raven's wings overhead. I quietly asked the spirit of the flowers to help guide Smudge and heal my lost soul. I picked all the flowers I could find, flowers Smudge might have tried to eat when she was alive: pink and white cosmos, daisies and rue leaves. I also picked blackberries, her favorite fruit, remembering how she would stand on her hind legs, plucking them like a small black bear.

I arrived at a special grove of cedar trees deep in the woods behind our house, a place where Jeff and I often meditated in the morning. I placed Smudge's body at the base of the largest of the trees, remembering that the Native Americans saw the cedar as the tree of life. I wondered how many tears the giant tree had witnessed. Decorating Smudge's body with flowers and placing the pile of berries beside her, I crossed her front feet and gently positioned her head as though she were sleeping. I lit a few small tea candles, surrounding her with light. The sweet aroma held me in the moment when I might have otherwise drifted into dreams of the past.

I smudged her body with sage, its powerful smoke circling around us, filling my empty heart. I did not want to let go. A deep sadness spread within me, permeating my marrow and lymph. For years, I had believed that when Smudge died, part of me would too, a part of me I liked, and I would be left with no choice but to hide in a closet. But now that the time was upon me, I saw no point in hiding. The pain would hunt me down and follow me in there too. She was and always will be my soul mate, that one dog who finds you only once in your life. As we shared our lives, we witnessed one another through many transformations, through many incarnations.

I sat beneath a giant cedar with Smudge's old grey body before me. In the chill of a summer morning, her spirit then leaped up at me, ran right up, barking in my face; she was so rebellious that way, so terrier-like when I would tell her "No!" And she just kept barking. I sat motionless, as we ran once again across the rolling fields of the Palouse, played hide-and-seek in the corn fields of Iowa, walked those freezing ice-covered nights along Lake Michigan in Chicago, and raced around Fresh Pond outside Boston. Like a guardian angel, Smudge had accompanied me through every turn of my life. At that point, I realized that nothing was permanent, nothing except my love for a terrier named Smudge.

People call it unconditional love, the way animals revere us and expect nothing in return. Jeff summed it up when he joined me in the cedar grove that morning, the smoke swirling around all three of us. "Love that expects nothing back. That is the real thing," he said, as he quietly sat next to me. Despite his calming words, my heart still raced and my thoughts rolled around in turmoil. What if I made the decision too hastily or too late? Perhaps I did not explore enough treatments that could have saved her.

Minutes ticked by but I didn't notice them. Birds sang in the trees as if nothing had happened, as if the world had not been shattered. Nature understood the cycle, but I was still angry at nature, angry at the way it paused for no one's sorrow. Later I would come to realize that, in all nature's cruelty and beauty, we are part of a changing world. Without death there can be no life. Nature doesn't judge. It just is.

It's hard to know how long I sat there. It could have been minutes or hours but the sun shifted several times. Trees I'd seen hundreds of times now loomed with a different sheen in the sun's golden rays. Mist rose into lofty streams of lime green lichen that hung in sheets from their branches. Jeff sat with the deep stillness of someone who's meditated for years. But for me, the passing of time hurt. My legs and back ached. My eyes burned although they were closed. And a dull headache traveled up and settled in my temples. I welcomed the pain I felt in my body because it started to alleviate the crippling pain I felt in my heart.

I opened my eyes. Just between the vine maple leaves, I saw a large ocean spray shrub, its tiny white flower clusters resembling an ocean's mist rising up as it crashes onto the shore. Its lobulated leaves stretched upward towards the sky like children's hands joyfully reaching for snowflakes. The flowers spiraled up from white frothy umbels, floating and exploding simultaneously. Each flower reminded me of tidal currents, governed by a gravitational pull so strong, it can feed a whole ecosystem and control global weather. Each ocean wave receded and expanded in a mesmerizing show of power, like a spirit leaving the shell of a body, its energy then dispersing back into sand, back into earth.

In life, Smudge gave the world no subtle messages. She ran circles around any other dog, living life to its fullest with each passing day. Like the crash of a wave against a rock, she left us all with a sense of exhilaration, a cold splash to wake us out of our thoughts and into *now*. With its spray-like flowers, the splendid plant broke through my sorrow, crashed up and soaked my face. And it felt every bit as good as that first cold nose in the morning.

Only the Beauty Remains

I HAD NURSED Tinkerbelle over the last several months, and after a brief period of improvement, she now continued to lose weight and was unwilling to eat without appetite stimulants, fluid therapy, B vitamins and plenty of coaxing. Although the treatments had prolonged her life, I knew that our time together was limited. At that point, I decided to take her back to Iris, knowing that her last days should be spent with her beloved companion. So we left Pullman and headed west towards Seattle, driving over the mountains in an early afternoon snowstorm. I had always imagined Tinkerbelle would live long enough to roam in the comfrey again. But sadly, I realized that was not going to happen.

Iris's life was also nearing its end. Standing by her bed, I could see it in her frail movements, in the stationary curve of her forefingers and in the pallor of her complexion. A hospice nurse came and went. The old woman's world was shrinking and now she only moved from her bed to the bathroom, occasionally sitting in her favorite armchair. As Iris slept, I lifted Tinkerbelle onto the pantry counter and gave her one last dose of fluids. Accustomed to my frequent doctoring, the cat sat perfectly still, her eyes gazing peacefully at mine. As I placed her on the bed beside Iris, she knew she was finally home and curled up in a comfortable ball in the crook of the old herbalist's elbow.

Upon waking, Iris mustered half a smile. Tinker began to purr. "Thank you for helping her," Iris whispered in a cracked voice, lifting her hand to stroke the cat. Even with Iris's raspy coughing, the cat did not move a muscle.

"Iris, see what I found?" I said, removing a cracked photo of Sampson from my cloth handbag and propping it beside her bed. "I never thanked you enough for curing him," I said, moving a tattered newspaper to sit in the old armchair, her cats' favorite perch. I remembered when Iris would have to shoo all of them off just so she could sit there herself. It was a chair worth fighting for. When Sampson was very sick, I cried in that same chair, holding the small dog in my lap. I felt as helpless now as I did then.

"Don't fiddle with the past," she said, slowly and softly. I tried to make sense of it all: her ailing cat, her own failing health and her unconventional teachings. Each was a strand in the intricate web of life. Just like my anatomy class, where I puzzled over the way the bones fit together to make a full skeleton, now I wondered how to put together all the pieces of Iris's life.

One late May afternoon, as she mumbled one of her lessons, we took on the arduous task of separating lemon balm from bee balm, the former prone to overtake the latter. "But it's pointless!" I protested, knocking my knee on a wheelbarrow. "We're never going to win this battle." The deep roots of new lemon balm plants encroached into the bee balm year after year. And year after year, my fingers ached from digging them out.

"But that is our job here on this planet," she said, chiseling beneath the roots. "We must protect the weaker plants and leave our small place on this planet better than when we found it." With each pass of her trowel, she let more light into the stunted bee balm, as if she could already see its magnificent red flowers. She described the hummingbirds that would feed from it, the sheen of their red and green feathers and the rapid flitting buzz of their wings.

I looked beyond the stale, dark bedroom to the garden she had created, where she had helped so many people and animals. I held Iris's cold hand with the unwavering grip of a terrier and placed my other hand gently on her sleeping cat as I clung to the memory of her many lessons over the years.

Not wanting to disturb their peaceful rest together, I slowly got up and stepped out into the gently falling snow. I looked up and let each cold, icy flake hit my face, fall into my eyes and salt my hair. Iris greeted each day with ardent anticipation, as though it were a brand new adventurous chapter, and I knew she would greet death that way too. I reached up to touch the snowflakes. I reached up to touch my life, and, at the same time, say goodbye to hers, touching the cycle in all its pain and beauty, over and over until only the beauty remained.

Epilogue

ON A BEAUTIFUL AUTUMN day, I step into my garden. The sun's low rays cast a golden hue upon each leaf. An occasional hummingbird dips into the bee balm. As I look at my sprawling patch of black cohosh, I see that it needs to be thinned in order to preserve its strength. I grab my favorite red-handled trowel from a bucket of hand tools. Scraping away the soil, I divide its knotted rhizomes into small pots. Kneeling under the canopy of fern-like leaves, I look up at each spike of white flowers. I trim small pieces of its roots and bring them into my herbal pharmacy. Placing them in the sink, I wash dirt away from the fresh roots and slice them up into small pieces to release their medicinal properties. Pouring alcohol over the crushed roots to create a dark brown tincture, I gaze up at the large amber bottles, each one neatly labeled, containing dried flowers, leaves, roots and powders, each holding a cure for my patients.

I then return to my garden to weed my echinacea beds: pink, purple and white coneflowers, the perfect balance of color and medicine. Behind me, I can hear the gentle hum of hundreds of honeybees surrounding the comfrey flowers, feeding from their rich healing nectar. Looking at the comfrey leaves, I think back to when Iris and I harvested them for Sampson's medicine. At one point early on, I had said to Iris, "Sometimes, I wonder if this tea is really helping him." Sampson then bounded away, chasing Tinkerbelle through the garden.

Iris stood firm, a handful of comfrey leaves in one hand and a rake in the other. And with the determination of a spirit who has lived many lifetimes, she directed her steadfast gaze towards the dog. "Donna, the proof is in that poodle."

Now, more than ever, I know she was right.

Acknowledgments

On Jeff's first edit, he saw the book as a cute, but flea-ridden, stray mutt. Due to his years in Western medicine, he figured all it needed was a little cleaning up and a good dose of a topical insecticide. But, of course, I chose the natural route, which involved hours of manual labor. So, for the next few weeks, we painstakingly used the editing version of a flea comb on our mangy patient. And after a period of time, out emerged a much cleaner, and hopefully flea-free, model. Although this dog may not have a pedigree, we hope you find it attractive nonetheless. And if you do happen to find a stray flea, please try to ignore it and keep reading. Thank you to my husband, Jeff Blake, for becoming my editor-in-chief.

The name Teshwintichina was borrowed from Jack Nisbet's brilliant book, *The Collector* (Sasquatch, 2009) about the fascinating life of David Douglas and his encounters with the original peoples of North America. Details about cooking camas bulb and other foods came from educational talks by Heidi Bohan, ethnobotanist and author of *The People of Cascadia*.

I also want to thank my other editors: Kate Ankofski of Hillcrest Media, Lynn Graham and Bill Smith, Bill Kueser and Greg Northcutt. Thanks to Carol Wells for her original art (you can check out her work at www.watercolorpetportraits.com); and to Mill City Press for helping me self-publish. Thank you to Al Pranke for my cover design. Thanks to the other two-leggeds: Madsu, Rosemary Gladstar, Michael Pilarski, KP Khalsa, Jeremy Ross, Adrienne Roan Bear and many others for their dedication to the preservation of herbal knowledge through the next generations. Other two-leggeds who deserve thanks: Robin Gates and Jill Hallin and Kelsy Smith for teaching me some of the complexities of the equine world. I thank my mother, Ann Kelleher, for teaching me the best way a parent can teach a child—by example—and for showing me that nothing can hold a woman back. Thanks also to my brother, Neil Kelleher, for putting up with a bunch of women who don't hold back. May his research help replace chemotherapy soon.

And last, but not least, thanks to my animals. The dogs:

Sampson, Julietta, Smudge, and Sugar Bear. The cats: Cirrus, Dolly Madison, Tigger, Tinkerbelle and let's not forget Gandalf the Grey. The rats: Saphire and Aphrodite. And Rufus Aspirilla, that incredible hamster. The horses: Lady Harlequin, Moses, Bill, Charlie, Chai, and Tino (also known as Scooter after his neuter). The elephants at Lek's Elephant Nature Foundation in Chiang Mai, Thailand, especially Jokia. Although she is blind, she still sees what good lies in all of us.

Thank you to my dedicated clients who put up with my limited appointment schedule. There are thousands of amazing animals I have had the honor of treating in the last seventeen years and I can only mention a few here. I salute these special animals, my patients, for everything you continue to teach me: Avalanche and Snowdrift, Yoshi, Razzle Dazzle, Binx, Pascal, Nandy and Georgie, Tucker, Jasper, Chacho, Ashley, Myles, Red Riley and Blue Bailey, Cosmo, Marley and Chicka, Maya, MacDuff and MacKenzie, Kodi, Sam, Winnie and Ping, Buddley and Zoe, Sadie and Dot, Frank and Shadow, Rosie, Burl, Tater Tot, Linus and Yum Yum, Kila, Harry, Sarah and Jules, Jackson, Belle and Buddy, Murphey, Jambo, Chloe and Parker, Alex, Phaze and Sarah, Nina, Sophie, Linus and Lucy, Nayo, Disco, Skye, Foozle and Reba, Roxie, Dexter and Lucy, Bonnie, Simba, Lightnin', Scout and Toby, Donnie and Abbey, Luka, Emmit, Kobi and Cole and Audrey, Jack and Joey, Tasha, Sadie and Sarah, Koyuk, Piper, Polla, Culio and Jazz, Jack, Darwin and Sirus, Chloe, Syri, Saba, Bertie, Phil, André, Serrano, Rudy and Jojo, Lucy, Maya and Hobbs, Woody and Scout, Ben, Reggie, Ella, Sasi, Caleb and Danny, Kacee, Lilly, Billie, Gracie, Maude, Jet Texas, Casey, Cassie, Katie, Tutt, Crickett, Mabel and Haus, Purrsia and Rodante, Max, Taz, Mingo, and the list goes on and on.

About the Author

Donna Kelleher graduated from Washington State University College of Veterinary Medicine in 1994. She is now certified by the International Veterinary Acupuncture Society and the American Veterinary Chiropractic Association and uses acupuncture, NAET, chiropractic, herbal medicine and nutrition to help treat animals with chronic conditions in her Seattle-based practice. Author of *The Last Chance Dog and Other True Stories of Holistic Animal Healing* (Scribner, 2003), she would love to see the day holistic medicine is offered as a first treatment option. She is a vegetarian, kayaker, gardener, tango dancer and horse companion. A member of the Washington Native Plant Society, she can often be found in the forest, investigating native plants.